D0110097

THE
AWAKENING

Kate Chopin

EDITORIAL DIRECTOR Justin Kestler
EXECUTIVE EDITOR Ben Florman
DIRECTOR OF TECHNOLOGY Tammy Hepps

SERIES EDITORS Boomie Aglietti, John Crowther, Justin Kestler
MANAGING EDITOR Vince Janoski

WRITERS Selena Ward, Sarah Spain
EDITORS Sarah Friedberg Katie Mannheimer

Copyright © 2002 by SparkNotes LLC

All rights reserved. No part of this book may be used or reproduced in any manner
whatsoever without the written permission of the Publisher.

SPARKNOTES is a registered trademark of SparkNotes LLC

This edition published by Spark Publishing

Spark Publishing
A Division of SparkNotes LLC
120 Fifth Avenue, 8th Floor
New York, NY 10011

Any book purchased without a cover is stolen property, reported as "unsold and
destroyed" to the Publisher, who receives no payment for such "stripped books."

03 04 05 SN 9 8 7 6 5 4 3 2

Please send all comments and questions or report errors to
litguides@sparknotes.com.

Library of Congress Catalog-in-Publication Data available upon request

Printed and bound in the United States

ISBN 1-58663-413-5

Introduction:
Stopping to Buy SparkNotes on a Snowy Evening

Whose words these are you *think* you know.
Your paper's due tomorrow, though;
We're glad to see you stopping here
To get some help before you go.

Lost your course? You'll find it here.
Face tests and essays without fear.
Between the words, good grades at stake:
Get great results throughout the year.

Once school bells caused your heart to quake
As teachers circled each mistake.
Use SparkNotes and no longer weep,
Ace every single test you take.

Yes, books are lovely, dark, and deep,
But only what you grasp you keep,
With hours to go before you sleep,
With hours to go before you sleep.

Contents

CONTEXT

KATE CHOPIN WAS BORN Catherine O'Flaherty on February 8, 1850, in St. Louis, Missouri. She was one of five children, but both her sisters died in infancy and her brothers died in their twenties. When she was five years old, Kate was sent to a Catholic boarding school named The Sacred Heart Academy. Just months later, however, her father died in a train accident, and she was sent home to live with her mother, grandmother, and great-grandmother, all widowed. After two years in their care, she returned to Sacred Heart, where she excelled in French and English, finishing at the top of her class.

Both at home with family and at school with the nuns, Kate grew up surrounded by intelligent and independent women. Her childhood lacked male role models; thus, she was rarely witness to the tradition of female submission and male domination that defined most late nineteenth-century marriages. The themes of female freedom and sexual awareness that dominated Chopin's adult writings were undoubtedly a result of the atmosphere in which she was raised.

After graduating from Sacred Heart, Kate became a part of the St. Louis social scene. In 1870 she married Oscar Chopin, the son of a prominent Creole family from Louisiana. Fulfilling the social responsibilities expected of her, Kate Chopin bore six children in the first ten years of her marriage to Oscar. Unlike many women of her time, however, she also enjoyed a wide range of unconventional freedoms. While Chopin was known to be a good wife and mother, she often grew tired of domestic life and escaped to smoke cigarettes or take solitary walks through New Orleans. She took strong, often controversial positions on the issues of the day. Chopin's husband loved her very deeply and supported and admired her independence and intelligence. She and her family lived happily in New Orleans for nine years.

When Oscar Chopin's cotton brokerage failed in 1879, he moved the family to Cloutierville, Louisiana, where he owned some land. Kate Chopin adjusted her habits easily to the smaller provincial lifestyle of Cloutierville and became the subject of much gossip. While other women in town were completing their household chores, Chopin would stroll or ride horseback down the town's main street, earning the attention and admiration of any man who passed her. In 1882, her husband died suddenly of swamp fever, leaving Chopin devastated. However, she would soon learn to enjoy the pleasures of independence and was rumored to have had an affair with a married neighbor, Albert Sampite, in the year following her husband's death. After a year spent managing her late husband's general store and plantation, Chopin moved back to Missouri with her children to be with her mother and family, a move that may have coincided with the end of her affair with Sampite. Sadly, Chopin's mother died shortly after her return, another in the series of tragic deaths that marked Kate's life.

In 1889 Chopin began writing fiction, an activity that enabled her to develop and express her strong views on women, sex, and marriage while simultaneously supporting her family. Chopin enjoyed immediate success with her writings about the French Creoles and Cajuns she had met and observed during her New Orleans and Cloutierville years. She sold dozens of short stories and essays exploring themes of love and independence, passion and freedom. By setting her stories in a specific region and community and by basing her characters on real people, Chopin was able to publish controversial stories in a socially acceptable format. Readers could choose to see the passions she described as curiosities of a localized culture rather than universalities in human nature. Chopin was often asked to attend conferences and give speeches and was widely celebrated for the majority of her short but prolific career.

Chopin's second and final novel, *The Awakening,* was published in 1899 at the height of her popularity. Ironically, this work, now regarded as a classic, essentially marked the end of Chopin's writing career. Many of Chopin's earlier works had been accepted despite their controversial subject matter because they appeared to contain narrative reporting rather than critical commentary. An underlying sense of support invaded the generally objective tone of *The Awakening,* however, and the reading public was shocked by such a sympathetic view toward the actions and emotions of the sexually aware and independent female protagonist.

The feminist movement, just beginning to emerge in other parts of America, was almost entirely absent in the conservative state of Louisiana. In fact, under Louisiana law, a woman was still considered the property of her husband. Chopin's novel was scorned and ostracized for its open discussion of the emotional and sexual needs of women. Surprised and deeply hurt by the negative reaction to *The*

Awakening, Chopin published only three more short stories before she died of a brain hemorrhage in 1904.

After her death, Chopin was remembered for her "local color" works about the people of New Orleans but was never acknowledged as a true literary talent until the rediscovery of *The Awakening* some fifty years later. New generations, more accepting of the notions of female sexuality and equality, praise the novel's candid and realistic views and have found it to be informative about early American feminism. Modern critics have noted the book's rich detail and imagery and find that its ironic narrative voice is a rich source for analysis. *The Awakening* has now earned a place in the literary canon for the way it uses these formal and structural techniques to explore themes of patriarchy, marriage and motherhood, woman's independence, desire, and sexuality both honestly and artistically.

Plot Overview

THE AWAKENING opens in the late 1800s in Grand Isle, a summer holiday resort popular with the wealthy inhabitants of nearby New Orleans. Edna Pontellier is vacationing with her husband, Léonce, and their two sons at the cottages of Madame Lebrun, which house affluent Creoles from the French Quarter. Léonce is kind and loving but preoccupied with his work. His frequent business-related absences mar his domestic life with Edna. Consequently, Edna spends most of her time with her friend Adèle Ratignolle, a married Creole who epitomizes womanly elegance and charm. Through her relationship with Adèle, Edna learns a great deal about freedom of expression. Because Creole women were expected and assumed to be chaste, they could behave in a forthright and unreserved manner. Exposure to such openness liberates Edna from her previously prudish behavior and repressed emotions and desires.

Edna's relationship with Adèle begins Edna's process of "awakening" and self-discovery, which constitutes the focus of the book. The process accelerates as Edna comes to know Robert Lebrun, the elder, single son of Madame Lebrun. Robert is known among the Grand Isle vacationers as a man who chooses one woman each year—often a married woman—to whom he then plays "attendant" all summer long. This summer, he devotes himself to Edna, and the two spend their days together lounging and talking by the shore. Adèle Ratignolle often accompanies them.

At first, the relationship between Robert and Edna is innocent. They mostly bathe in the sea or engage in idle talk. As the summer progresses, however, Edna and Robert grow closer, and Robert's affections and attention inspire in Edna several internal revelations. She feels more alive than ever before, and she starts to paint again as she did in her youth. She also learns to swim and becomes aware of her independence and sexuality. Edna and Robert never openly discuss their love for one another, but the time they spend alone together kindles memories in Edna of the dreams and desires of her youth. She becomes inexplicably depressed at night with her husband and profoundly joyful during her moments of freedom, whether alone or with Robert. Recognizing how intense the relationship between him and Edna has become, Robert honorably

4

removes himself from Grand Isle to avoid consummating his forbidden love. Edna returns to New Orleans a changed woman.

Back in New Orleans, Edna actively pursues her painting and ignores all of her social responsibilities. Worried about the changing attitude and increasing disobedience of his wife, Léonce seeks the guidance of the family physician, Doctor Mandelet. A wise and enlightened man, Doctor Mandelet suspects that Edna's transformation is the result of an affair, but he hides his suspicions from Léonce. Instead, Doctor Mandelet suggests that Léonce let Edna's defiance run its course, since attempts to control her would only fuel her rebellion. Léonce heeds the doctor's advice, allowing Edna to remain home alone while he is away on business. With her husband gone and her children away as well, Edna wholly rejects her former lifestyle. She moves into a home of her own and declares herself independent—the possession of no one. Her love for Robert still intense, Edna pursues an affair with the town seducer, Alcée Arobin, who is able to satisfy her sexual needs. Never emotionally attached to Arobin, Edna maintains control throughout their affair, satisfying her animalistic urges but retaining her freedom from male domination.

At this point, the self-sufficient and unconventional old pianist Mademoiselle Reisz adopts Edna as a sort of protégé, warning Edna of the sacrifices required of an artist. Edna is moved by Mademoiselle Reisz's piano playing and visits her often. She is also eager to read the letters from abroad that Robert sends the woman. A woman who devotes her life entirely to her art, Mademoiselle serves as an inspiration and model to Edna, who continues her process of awakening and independence. Mademoiselle Reisz is the only person who knows of Robert and Edna's secret love for one another and she encourages Edna to admit to, and act upon, her feelings.

Unable to stay away, Robert returns to New Orleans, finally expressing openly his feelings for Edna. He admits his love but reminds her that they cannot possibly be together, since she is the wife of another man. Edna explains to him her newly established independence, denying the rights of her husband over her and explaining how she and Robert can live together happily, ignoring everything extraneous to their relationship. But despite his love for Edna, Robert feels unable to enter into the adulterous affair.

When Adèle undergoes a difficult and dangerous childbirth, Edna leaves Robert's arms to go to her friend. She pleads with him to wait for her return. From the time she spends with Edna, Adèle senses that Edna is becoming increasingly distant, and she understands that Edna's relationship with Robert has intensified. She reminds Edna to think of her children and advocates the socially acceptable lifestyle Edna abandoned so long ago. Doctor Mandelet, while walking Edna home from Adèle's, urges her to come see him because he is worried about the outcome of her passionate but confused actions. Already reeling under the weight of Adèle's admonition, Edna begins to perceive herself as having acted selfishly.

Edna returns to her house to find Robert gone, a note of farewell left in his place. Robert's inability to escape the ties of society now prompts Edna's most devastating awakening. Haunted by thoughts of her children and realizing that she would have eventually found even Robert unable to fulfill her desires and dreams, Edna feels an overwhelming sense of solitude. Alone in a world in which she has found no feeling of belonging, she can find only one answer to the inescapable and heartbreaking limitations of society. She returns to Grand Isle, the site of her first moments of emotional, sexual, and intellectual awareness, and, in a final escape, gives herself to the sea. As she swims through the soft, embracing water, she thinks about her freedom from her husband and children, as well as Robert's failure to understand her, Doctor Mandelet's words of wisdom, and Mademoiselle Reisz's courage. The text leaves open the question of whether the suicide constitutes a cowardly surrender or a liberating triumph.

CHARACTER LIST

Edna Pontellier Edna is the protagonist of the novel, and the "awakening" to which the title refers is hers. The twenty-eight-year-old wife of a New Orleans businessman, Edna suddenly finds herself dissatisfied with her marriage and the limited, conservative lifestyle that it allows. She emerges from her semi-conscious state of devoted wife and mother to a state of total awareness, in which she discovers her own identity and acts on her desires for emotional and sexual satisfaction. Through a series of experiences, or "awakenings," Edna becomes a shockingly independent woman, who lives apart from her husband and children and is responsible only to her own urges and passions. Tragically, Edna's awakenings isolate her from others and ultimately lead her to a state of total solitude.

Mademoiselle Reisz Mademoiselle Reisz may be the most influential character in Edna's awakening. She is unmarried and childless, and she devotes her life to her passion: music. A talented pianist and somewhat of a recluse, she represents independence and freedom and serves as a sort of muse for Edna. When Edna begins actively to pursue personal independence, she seeks Mademoiselle Reisz's companionship. Mademoiselle warns Edna that she must be brave if she wishes to be an artist—that an artist must have a courageous and defiant soul. Mademoiselle Reisz is the only character in the novel who knows of the love between Robert and Edna, and she, thus, serves as a true confidante for Edna despite their considerably different personalities. Mademoiselle Reisz is also a foil for Edna's other close female friend, Adèle Ratignolle, who epitomizes the conventional and socially acceptable woman of the late nineteenth century.

Adèle Ratignolle Edna's close friend, Adèle Ratignolle represents the Victorian feminine ideal. She idolizes her children and worships her husband, centering her life around caring for them and performing her domestic duties. While her lifestyle and attitude contrast with Edna's increasing independence, Adèle unwittingly helps facilitate her friend's transformation. Her free manner of discourse and expression, typical of Creole women of the time, acts as a catalyst for Edna's abandonment of her former reserved and introverted nature. Adele is also a foil for Mademoiselle Reisz, whose independent and unconventional lifestyle inspires Edna's transgressions.

Robert Lebrun Robert Lebrun is the twenty-six-year-old single man with whom Edna falls in love. Dramatic and passionate, he has a history of becoming the devoted attendant to a different woman each summer at Grand Isle. Robert offers his affections comically and in an over-exaggerated manner, and thus is never taken seriously. As the friendship between Robert and Edna becomes more intimate and complex, however, he realizes that he has genuinely fallen in love with Edna. He is torn between his love for her and society's view that women are the possessions of their husbands.

Alcée Arobin The seductive, charming, and forthright Alcée Arobin is the Don Juan of the New Orleans Creole community. Arobin enjoys making conquests out of married women, and he becomes Edna's lover while her husband is on a business trip to New York. Although Robert Lebrun is the man whom Edna truly loves, Arobin satisfies Edna's physical urges while Robert is in Mexico. Throughout their passionate affair, Edna retains authority and never allows Alcée to own or control her.

Léonce Pontellier Léonce Pontellier, a forty-year-old, wealthy New Orleans businessman, is Edna's husband. Although he loves Edna and his sons, he spends little time with them because he is often away on business or with his friends. Very concerned with social appearances, Léonce wishes Edna to continue the practices expected of New Orleans women despite her obvious distaste for them. He treats Edna with love and kindness, but their relationship lacks passion and excitement, and he knows very little of his wife's true feelings and emotions.

Doctor Mandelet Doctor Mandelet is Léonce and Edna's family physician. He is a fairly enlightened man, who silently recognizes Edna's dissatisfaction with the restrictions placed on her by social conventions. When Léonce consults with him about Edna's unconventional behavior, the doctor suspects that Edna is in love with another man, although he keeps his suspicions to himself because he recognizes that there is little Léonce can do if Edna is indeed in love with someone else and that any further constraints imposed on her will only intensify her revolt. Doctor Mandelet offers Edna his help and understanding and is worried about the possible consequences of her defiance and independence.

The Colonel The Colonel, a former Confederate officer in the Civil War, is Edna's father. He is a strict Protestant and believes that husbands should manage their wives with authority and coercion. While Edna's relationship with her father is not affectionate, she is surprised by how well she gets along with her father when they are together.

Victor Lebrun Victor Lebrun is Robert's wayward younger brother. He spends his time chasing women and refuses to settle down into a profession.

CHARACTER LIST

Madame Lebrun Madame Lebrun is the widowed mother of Victor and Robert. She owns and manages the cottages on Grand Isle where the novel's characters spend their summer vacations.

The Lady in Black The lady in black is a vacationer at the Lebrun cottages on Grand Isle. She embodies the patient, resigned solitude that convention expects of a woman whose husband has died, but her solitude does not speak to any sort of independence or strength. Rather, it owes to a self-effacing withdrawal from life and passion out of utter respect for her husband's death. Throughout the novel, the lady in black remains silent, which contributes to her lack of individuality and to her role within the text as the symbol of the socially acceptable husbandless woman.

The Two Lovers The two lovers are vacationers at the Lebrun cottages on Grand Isle. They represent the form of young love accepted by society. Always appearing in conjunction with the lady in black, the lovers represent the stage of a woman's life that precedes her maternal duties.

The Farival Twins The Farival twins are fourteen-year-old girls who vacation at Grand Isle with their family and who frequently entertain their fellow guests by playing the piano. They represent the destiny of adolescent Victorian girls: chaste motherhood. Having been dedicated to the Virgin Mary at birth, they wear her colors at all times. Moreover, they embody society's expectations of the way women should use art—as a way of making themselves more delightful to others, rather than as a means of self-expression.

Mrs. Highcamp A tall, worldly woman in her forties, Mrs. Highcamp spends time with many of the fashionable single men of New Orleans under the pretext of finding a husband for her daughter. Alcée Arobin is one of these young men, and the two call on Edna to attend the races and to accompany them to dinner—meetings that catalyze the affair between Edna and Arobin.

Janet and Margaret Pontellier Janet is Edna's younger sister. Edna was never close to her and she refuses to attend her wedding. Margaret is Edna and Janet's older sister. After their mother died, Margaret took over the role of mother figure for her younger sisters.

Mariequita A young, pretty Spanish girl, Mariequita is a mischievous flirt who lives on Grand Isle. She seems to fancy both Robert and Victor Lebrun and, along with Adèle, is the picture of the self-demeaning coquetry that Edna avoids.

Madame Antoine When Edna feels faint at the Sunday service on the island of *Chênière Caminada,* she and Robert go to Madame Antoine's for the day. A friendly inhabitant of the island, Madame Antoine takes them in and cares for Edna, to whom she tells stories of her life.

Mr. and Mrs. Merriman, Miss Mayblunt, & Mr. Gouvernail Some of the guests present at the dinner party Edna holds to celebrate her move to the "pigeon house."

Etienne & Raoul Pontellier Etienne and Raoul are Edna and Léonce's two sons. They are four and five years old, respectively.

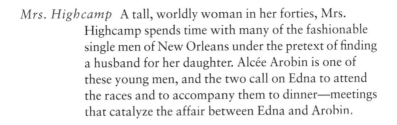

CHARACTER LIST

ANALYSIS OF MAJOR CHARACTERS

EDNA PONTELLIER

Edna Pontellier is a respectable woman of the late 1800s who not only acknowledges her sexual desires, but also has the strength and courage to act on them. Breaking through the role appointed to her by society, she discovers her own identity independent of her husband and children. Many of Kate Chopin's other stories feature passionate, unconventional female protagonists, but none presents a heroine as openly rebellious as Edna. The details and specifics of Edna's character are key to understanding the novel and its impact on generations of readers.

At the beginning of the novel, Edna exists in a sort of semi-conscious state. She is comfortable in her marriage to Léonce and unaware of her own feelings and ambitions. Edna has always been a romantic, enamored with a cavalry officer at a very young age, in love with a man visiting a neighboring plantation in her teens, and infatuated with a tragedian as a young woman. But she saw her marriage to Léonce as the end to her life of passion and the beginning of a life of responsibility. Although she expected her dreams of romance to disappear along with her youth, her fantasies and yearnings only remain latent, re-emerging on Grand Isle in the form of her passion for Robert Lebrun.

The people Edna meets and the experiences she has on Grand Isle awaken desires and urges for music, sexual satisfaction, art, and freedom that she can no longer bear to keep hidden. Like a child, Edna begins to see the world around her with a fresh perspective, forgetting the behavior expected of her and ignoring the effects of her unconventional actions. Yet Edna is often childish as well as childlike: she harbors unrealistic dreams about the possibilities of a wild adulterous romance without consequences, and she fails to consider the needs and desires of anyone but herself. Her flagrant disregard of reality is revealed when she mocks Robert's apprehensions about adultery, and when she leaves her children in the care of their grandmother without a second thought. Edna's independence frequently amounts to selfishness.

Yet although the text never presents Edna's escape from tradition as heroic, it also never declares her actions shameful. The narrative may sometimes portray Edna as selfish in the ways she acts out her defiance of convention, but it never portrays Edna's defiance itself as intrinsically wrong. Perhaps, even, the novel portrays Edna's rebellion as intrinsically right. Given the book's ambiguity, Edna's decision to commit suicide at the end of the novel can be read either as an act of cowardice—of submission to thoughts of her sons' reputations and to a sense that life has become too difficult—or as an act of final rebellion—of refusal to sacrifice her integrity by putting her life in the hands of controlling powers.

MADEMOISELLE REISZ

Mademoiselle Reisz is an unconventional and unpopular older woman who serves as an inspiration to Edna throughout her gradual awakening. A small, homely woman, Mademoiselle is distant and reserved in her interaction with the other guests on Grand Isle. Although she is often called upon to entertain people at gatherings with her expert piano playing, she realizes that Edna is the only one of the guests who is truly touched and moved by the music. Mademoiselle Reisz seeks out Edna shortly after Robert's departure to Mexico, and her exchange with Edna by the shore fosters a relationship that continues upon their return home to New Orleans. Edna is inexplicably drawn to the older woman, whose lifestyle she envies, despite finding her disagreeable and difficult. In fact, neither Edna nor Mademoiselle Reisz can claim to be particularly fond of the other, but Mademoiselle Reisz understands Edna's passions and enjoys the company and the opportunity to share her thoughts on art and love.

Through her relationship with the pianist, Edna increases her awareness of herself as a woman capable of passionate art and passionate love. While the two capacities are interconnected, Mademoiselle Reisz serves to further each specifically. Not only is the pianist in touch with her own artistic emotions, she is, on a more pragmatic level, in touch with the traveling Robert and is the only one to whom he speaks of his love for Edna.

Mademoiselle Reisz is the woman that Edna could have become, had she lived into her old age and remained independent of her husband and children. Mademoiselle functions as a sort of muse for her young companion, acting as a living example of an entirely self-sufficient woman, who is ruled by her art and her passions, rather than by the expectations of society. Mademoiselle Reisz acts as a foil for Adèle Ratignolle, who lives the socially accepted lifestyle that Mademoiselle Reisz rejected for solitude and freedom.

ADÈLE RATIGNOLLE

A foil for Mademoiselle Reisz, Adèle is a devoted wife and mother, the epitome of nineteenth-century womanhood. Adèle spends her days caring for her children, performing her domestic duties, and ensuring the happiness of her husband. Ironically, while Adèle is comfortable and happy with her simple, conformist existence, she unintentionally catalyzes Edna's movement away from such a life-style with her manner of speech: because she and her fellow Creole women are so clearly chaste and irreproachably moral, society allows them to speak openly on such matters as pregnancy, under-garments, and romantic gossip. Adèle's conversation reminds Edna of the romantic dreams and fantasies of her youth, and Edna gradu-ally begins to uncover the desires that had been suppressed for so many years. Although Adèle's behavior represents that which is expected of Edna, the effect of her words proves more powerful than her example.

Adèle is a static character—she shows no change or growth from the beginning of the novel to its end. She is also somewhat simple: when Edna reveals to Adèle that she would give up her money and her life for her children but not herself, Adèle cannot understand what more one could give than one's own life. Edna's understanding of an inner, autonomous spirit defies the belief of the time that women were simply the property of their husbands, who served a specific role as wives and mothers and devoted themselves solely to those around them at their own expense. Later in the novel, it is apparent that Adèle still views a woman's life in terms of the service she performs for her family and society. When she suspects Edna of having an affair with Alcée Arobin she reminds Edna of her duty to her children. Having just given birth to another child, Adèle still rep-resents the ideal Victorian woman, whereas Edna ignores her responsibilities to husband and children, seeking freedom up until, or perhaps even through, her death.

ROBERT LEBRUN

Although he remains away in Mexico for much of Edna's awakening, Robert Lebrun plays an invaluable role in its beginning and end. His flirtations, along with Adèle's freedom of expression, inspire Edna to forget her reserve and to begin revealing herself to others. For several summers, Robert has devoted himself to women at Grand Isle, showering them with affections rooted in admiration but lacking serious intent. Although notoriously ruled by his passions and impulses, he nevertheless cannot forget the societal conventions that both allow and limit his actions. Unlike the Creole women who play along with his flirtations, enjoying the company and attention, Edna is swept away by Robert's devotion. She sees in him a promise of the love and excitement that have been missing from her life since she married Léonce. Although he never consummates their relationship physically, Robert's tender treatment of Edna proves that his love for her extends beyond the superficial adoration he is used to showing his female companions. When Robert recognizes the intensity of his feelings for Edna, he decides to go to Mexico because he cannot bear to be near Edna and know that he may never act on his love.

Robert's courtship of Edna on Grand Isle perches precariously on the boundary between innocence and misconduct, suggesting that defiance and daring may lie beneath his reputation as a harmless flirt. Robert's sudden return from Mexico and his unrealistic plan to request that Léonce set Edna free so that Robert may make her his wife manifest a bolder side to Robert's nature. However, Robert pragmatically recognizes the difference between daydream and reality. When he returns to New Orleans, he accepts the impossibility of his intentions, and he ignores Edna's claims of independence and self-ownership. Despite his sincere love and urgent lust, Robert cannot, as Edna has, escape from or ignore the rules of society. The note he leaves when he flees her house sums up for Edna the unjust, unchangeable state of the world around her. Robert's ultimate fidelity to convention and society solidifies her disappointment with life and with the role she is expected to play. While Edna despairs over Robert's rejection of her, her suicide is not a response to her disappointment but rather to the final awakening that it affords her. When even Robert, whose love matches the sincerity and desperation of her own, will not trespass the boundaries of societal convention, Edna acknowledges the profundity of her solitude.

THEMES, MOTIFS & SYMBOLS

THEMES

Themes are the fundamental and often universal ideas explored in a literary work.

SOLITUDE AS THE CONSEQUENCE OF INDEPENDENCE

For Edna Pontellier, the protagonist of *The Awakening,* independence and solitude are almost inseparable. The expectations of tradition coupled with the limitations of law gave women of the late 1800s very few opportunities for individual expression, not to mention independence. Expected to perform their domestic duties and care for the health and happiness of their families, Victorian women were prevented from seeking the satisfaction of their own wants and needs. During her gradual awakening, Edna discovers her own identity and acknowledges her emotional and sexual desires.

Initially, Edna experiences her independence as no more than an emotion. When she swims for the first time, she discovers her own strength, and through her pursuit of her painting she is reminded of the pleasure of individual creation. Yet when Edna begins to verbalize her feelings of independence, she soon meets resistance from the constraints—most notably, her husband—that weigh on her active life. And when she makes the decision to abandon her former lifestyle, Edna realizes that independent ideas cannot always translate into a simultaneously self-sufficient and socially acceptable existence.

Ultimately, the passion that Robert feels for Edna is not strong enough to join the lovers in a true union of minds, since although Robert's passion is strong enough to make him feel torn between his love and his sense of moral rectitude, it is not strong enough to make him decide in favor of his love. The note Robert leaves for Edna makes clear to Edna the fact that she is ultimately alone in her awakening. Once Robert refuses to trespass the boundaries of societal convention, Edna acknowledges the profundity of her solitude.

THE IMPLICATIONS OF SELF-EXPRESSION

Edna's discovery of ways to express herself leads to the revelation of her long-repressed emotions. During her awakening, Edna learns at least three new "languages." First, she learns the mode of expression of the Creole women on Grand Isle. Despite their chastity, these women speak freely and share their emotions openly. Their frankness initially shocks Edna, but she soon finds it liberating. Edna learns that she can face her emotions and sexuality directly, without fear. Once her Creole friends show her that it is okay to speak and think about one's own feelings, Edna begins to acknowledge, name, define, and articulate her emotions.

Edna also learns to express herself through art. This lesson occurs in Chapter IX, when Edna hears Mademoiselle Reisz perform on the piano. Whereas previously music had called up images to her mind, the mademoiselle's piano playing stirs her in a deeper way: "she saw no pictures of solitude, of hope, of longing, or of despair. But the very passions themselves were aroused within her soul, swaying it, lashing it, as the waves daily beat upon her splendid body." As the music ceases to conjure up images in Edna mind, it becomes for Edna a sort of call to something within herself. Additionally, Mademoiselle Reisz has felt that she and Edna have been communicating through the music: noting Edna's "agitation," she says that Edna is "the only one" at the party who is "worth playing for." Once Edna is aware of music's power to express emotion, she begins to paint as she has never painted before. Painting ceases to be a diversion and becomes instead a form of true expression.

From Robert and Alcée, Edna learns how to express the love and passion she has kept secret for so long. As with her other processes of language-learning, Edna finds that once she learns the "vocabulary" with which to express her needs and desires, she is better able to define them for herself. A pattern emerges—Edna can learn a language from a person but then surpass her teacher's use of her newfound form of expression. For example, while Adèle teaches her that they can be open with one another, Edna soon wants to apply this frankness to all areas of her life. And although Robert helps to teach her the language of sexuality, she wants to speak this language loudly, as it were, while Robert still feels social pressure to whisper.

As Edna's ability to express herself grows, the number of people who can understand her newfound languages shrinks. Ultimately, Edna's suicide is linked to a dearth of people who can truly understand and empathize with her. Especially after Robert's rejection of her in Chapter XXXVIII, Edna is convinced definitively of her essential solitude because the language of convention Robert speaks has become incomprehensible to Edna. Although Robert has taught her the language of sexuality, Edna has become too fluent. In this dilemma, Edna mirrors the parrot in Chapter I, which speaks French and "a little Spanish" but "also a language which nobody understood, unless it was the mocking-bird. . . ." The mockingbird, which merely whistles inarticulate "fluty notes" with "maddening persistence," resembles Edna's friends who seem to understand Edna but do not speak back.

MOTIFS

Motifs are recurring structures, contrasts, or literary devices that can help to develop and inform the text's major themes.

MUSIC

Throughout *The Awakening,* the manner in which each of the characters uses and understands music gives us a sense of Edna's ideological alignment in relation to the novel's other characters. Additionally, Edna's exploration of music and her meditations upon its significance enable her own (visual) art to flourish. Edna first learns about the emotive power of music from Mademoiselle Reisz. Whereas Adèle Ratignolle's piano playing had merely conjured sentimental pictures for Edna, the older woman's playing stirs new feelings and probes unexplored emotional territories in her. Mademoiselle Reisz uses music as a form of artistic expression, not merely as a way of entertaining others. In contrast to Mademoiselle Reisz, the Farival twins play the piano purely for the sake of the gathered company. The twins' association with the Virgin Mary, and, hence, with a destiny of chaste motherliness, links them thematically with notions of how Victorian women should behave. Their piano playing—entertaining but not provocative, pleasant but not challenging—similarly serves as the model for how women *should* use art. It becomes clear that, for a Victorian woman, the use of art as a form of self-exploration and self-articulation constitutes a rebellion. Correspondingly, Mademoiselle Reisz's use of music situates her as a nonconformist and a sympathetic confidante for Edna's awakening.

The difference Edna detects between the piano-playing of Mademoiselle Reisz and Adèle Ratignolle seems also to testify to Edna's emotional growth. She reaches a point in her awakening in which she is able to hear what a piece of music says to her, rather than idly inventing random pictures to accompany the sounds. Thus, music, or Edna's changing reactions to it, also serves to help the reader locate Edna in her development.

CHILDREN

Images of children, and verbal allusions to them, occur throughout the novel. Edna herself is often metaphorically related to a child. In her awakening, she is undergoing a form of rebirth as she discovers the world from a fresh, childlike, perspective. Yet Edna's childishness has a less admirable side. Edna becomes self-absorbed, she disregards others, and she fails to think realistically about the future or to meditate on her the consequences of her actions.

Ultimately, Edna's thoughts of her children inspire her to commit suicide, because she realizes that no matter how little she depends on others, her children's lives will always be affected by society's opinion of her. Moreover, her children represent an obligation that, unlike Edna's obligation to her husband, is irrevocable. Because children are so closely linked to Edna's suicide, her increasing allusions to "the little lives" of her children prefigure her tragic end.

HOUSES

Edna stays in many houses in *The Awakening*: the cottages on Grand Isle, Madame Antoine's home on the *Chênière Caminada,* the big house in New Orleans, and her "pigeon house." Each of these houses serves as a marker of her progress as she undergoes her awakening. Edna is expected to be a "mother-woman" on Grand Isle, and to be the perfect social hostess in New Orleans. While she is living in the cottage on Grand Isle and in the big house in New Orleans, Edna maintains stays within the "walls" of these traditional roles and does not look beyond them.

However, when she and Robert slip away to the *Chênière Caminada*, their temporary rest in Madame Antoine's house symbolizes the shift that Edna has undergone. Staying in the house, Edna finds herself in a new, romantic, and foreign world. It is as though the old social structures must have disappeared, and on this new island Edna can forget the other guests on Grand Isle and create a world of her own. Significantly, Madame Antoine's house serves only as a temporary shelter—it is not a "home." Edna's newfound world of liberty is not a place where she can remain.

The "pigeon house" does allow Edna to be both at "home" and independent. Once she moves to the pigeon house, Edna no longer has to look at the material objects that Léonce has purchased and with which Edna equates herself. She can behave as she likes, without regard to how others will view her actions. In the end, however, the little house will prove not to be the solution Edna expected. While it does provide her with independence and isolation, allowing her to progress in her sexual awakening and to escape the gilded cage that Léonce's house constituted, Edna finds herself cooped anew, if less extravagantly. The fact that her final house resembles those used to keep domesticated pigeons does not bode well for Edna's fate. In the end, feeling alternately an exile and a prisoner, she is "at home" nowhere. Only in death can she hope to find the things a home offers—respite, privacy, shelter, and comfort.

SYMBOLS

Symbols are objects, characters, figures, or colors used to represent abstract ideas or concepts.

BIRDS

In The Awakening, caged birds serve as reminders of Edna's entrapment and also of the entrapment of Victorian women in general. Madame Lebrun's parrot and mockingbird represent Edna and Madame Reisz, respectively. Like the birds, the women's movements are limited (by society), and they are unable to communicate with the world around them. The novel's "winged" women may only use their wings to protect and shield, never to fly.

Edna's attempts to escape her husband, children, and society manifest this arrested flight, as her efforts only land her in another cage: the pigeon house. While Edna views her new home as a sign of her independence, the pigeon house represents her inability to remove herself from her former life, as her move takes her just "two steps away." Mademoiselle Reisz instructs Edna that she must have strong wings in order to survive the difficulties she will face if she plans to act on her love for Robert. She warns: "The bird that would soar above the level plain of tradition and prejudice must have strong wings. It is a sad spectacle to see the weaklings bruised, exhausted, fluttering back to earth."

Critics who argue that Edna's suicide marks defeat, both individually and for women, point out the similar wording of the novel's final example of bird imagery: "A bird with a broken wing was beating the air above, reeling, fluttering, circling disabled down, down to the water." If, however, the bird is not a symbol of Edna herself, but rather of Victorian womanhood in general, then its fall represents the fall of convention achieved by Edna's suicide.

THE SEA

The sea in *The Awakening* symbolizes freedom and escape. It is a vast expanse that Edna can brave only when she is solitary and only after she has discovered her own strength. When in the water, Edna is reminded of the depth of the universe and of her own position as a human being within that depth. The sensuous sound of the surf constantly beckons and seduces Edna throughout the novel.

Water's associations with cleansing and baptism make it a symbol of rebirth. The sea, thus, also serves as a reminder of the fact that Edna's awakening is a rebirth of sorts. Appropriately, Edna ends her life in the sea: a space of infinite potential becomes a blank and enveloping void that carries both a promise and a threat. In its sublime vastness, the sea represents the strength, glory, and lonely horror of independence.

SYMBOLS

SUMMARY & ANALYSIS

CHAPTERS I–V

SUMMARY: CHAPTER I

The novel opens on Grand Isle, a summer retreat for the wealthy French Creoles of New Orleans. Léonce Pontellier, a wealthy New Orleans businessman of forty, reads his newspaper outside the Isle's main guesthouse. Two birds, the pets of the guesthouse's proprietor, Madame Lebrun, are making a great deal of noise. The parrot repeats phrases in English and French while the mockingbird sings persistently. Hoping to escape the birds' disruptive chatter, Léonce retreats into the cottage he has rented. Glancing back at the main building, Léonce notes that the noise emanating from it has increased: the Farival twins play the piano, Madame Lebrun gives orders to two servants, and a lady in black walks back and forth with her rosary beads in hand. Down by the water-oaks his four-and five-year-old sons play under the watchful eye of their quadroon (one-quarter black) nurse.

Léonce smokes a cigar and watches as his wife, Edna, strolls toward him from the beach, accompanied by the young Robert Lebrun, Mrs. Lebrun's son. Léonce notices that his wife is sunburned and scolds her for swimming during the hottest hours of the day. He returns the rings he's been holding for Edna and invites Robert to play some billiards at Klein's hotel. Robert declines and stays to talk with Edna as Léonce walks away.

SUMMARY: CHAPTER II

Robert and Edna talk without pause, discussing the sights and people around them. Robert, a clean-shaven, carefree young man, discusses his plans to seek his fortune in Mexico at the end of the summer. Edna is handsome and engaging. She talks about her childhood in Kentucky bluegrass country and her sister's upcoming wedding.

SUMMARY: CHAPTER III

Léonce is in great spirits when he returns from playing billiards late that evening. He wakes Edna to tell her the news and gossip from the club, and he is disappointed when she responds with groggy half-answers. He goes to check on his sons and informs Edna that Raoul

SUMMARY & ANALYSIS

seems to have a fever. She replies that the child was fine when he went to bed, but Léonce insists that she attend to him, criticizing Edna for her "habitual neglect of the children."

After a cursory visit to the boys' bedroom, Edna returns to bed, refusing to answer any of her husband's inquiries. Léonce soon falls asleep but Edna remains wide awake. She sits on the porch and weeps quietly as she listens to the sea. Though she has found herself inexplicably unhappy many times before, she has always felt comforted by the kindness and devotion of her husband. This particular evening, however, Edna experiences an unfamiliar oppression. It fills her "whole being" and keeps her out on the porch until the bugs force her back inside.

The next morning, Léonce departs for a week-long business trip. Before he leaves, he gives Edna some spending money and says goodbye to the small crowd that has gathered to see him off. From New Orleans, he sends Edna a box of bonbons that she shares with her friends. All of the ladies declare Léonce the best husband in the world, and under pressure Edna admits "she kn[ows] of none better."

SUMMARY: CHAPTER IV

Léonce cannot explain why he always feels dissatisfied with Edna's treatment of their sons, but he perceives a difference between his wife and the other women on Grand Isle. Unlike the others, who are "mother-women," Edna does not "idolize" her children or "worship" her husband at the cost of her own individuality. Edna's friend Adèle Ratignolle, who embodies all the grace and charm of a romantic heroine, is the prime example of the mother-woman. Back on Grand Isle, Adèle, Edna, and Robert relax, eating the bonbons Léonce has sent and conversing about Adèle's sewing, the chocolates, and, much to Edna's shock, childbirth. As a result of her marriage to Léonce, who is a Creole (a person descended from the original French and Spanish settlers of New Orleans, an aristocrat), Edna has spent a great deal of time surrounded by Creole women. Yet, she is still not entirely comfortable with their customs. Their lack of self-restraint in conversation is at odds with mainstream American conventions. Nevertheless, they somehow possess a quality of lofty purity that seems to keep them free of reproach.

SUMMARY: CHAPTER V

Since early adolescence, Robert has chosen one woman each summer to whom he devotes himself as an attendant. As he sits with Edna and Adèle by the shore, he tells Edna of his days as Adèle's attendant. Adèle jests that, at the time, she had feared her husband's jealousy, a comment that inspires laughter because it was accepted that a Creole husband never has reason to be jealous. Adèle says that she never took Robert's proclamations of love as serious confessions of passion.

Robert's decision to devote himself to Edna for the summer comes as no surprise to those on Grand Isle. Yet although Robert devotes himself to a different woman every summer, his playful attentions to Edna differ from his treatments of past women, and when he and Edna are alone he never speaks of love in the same "serio-comic tone" he used with Adèle. Edna sketches Adèle while Robert watches. He leans his head on Edna's arm until she gently pushes him away. Adèle is disappointed that the finished drawing does not resemble her, but she is still pleased by the work. Edna herself is unsatisfied. She smudges the paint and crumples the drawing.

Edna's children bound up the steps with their nurse some distance behind them. They help Edna bring her painting equipment into the house and she rewards them with bonbons before they scamper away again. Adèle experiences a brief fainting spell, which Edna suspects may be feigned. After recovering, Adèle gracefully retires to her cottage, meeting her own three children along the way and receiving them with "a thousand endearments." Edna declines Robert's suggestion that they go for a swim, unconvincingly complaining that she is too tired. She soon gives in to Robert's insistent entreaties, however, and he places her straw hat on her head as they move toward the beach.

Analysis: Chapters I–V

It is appropriate that *The Awakening,* which is essentially a novel about the social constraints of women in the Victorian era, opens with the shrieking complaint of a constrained parrot: "Go away! Go away! For God's sake." These words, the first in *The Awakening,* immediately hint at the tragic nature of the novel, as the bird echoes the phrases of rejection and rebuff that it has heard time and again. Although Madame Lebrun's parrot speaks English, French, and "a little Spanish," it also speaks a "language which nobody understood, unless it was the mocking-bird that hung on the other side of the door, whistling his fluty notes. . . ." Caged and misunderstood, the parrot's predicament mirrors Edna's.

Edna also speaks a language that nobody, not even her husband, friends, or lovers, understands. It seems that Edna must have a mockingbird-type figure, someone who understands her mysterious language as the mockingbird understands the parrot's. Although we have not yet met her, it will soon become clear that, if the parrot stands for Edna, the mockingbird represents Mademoiselle Reisz, the unconventional and self-sufficient pianist who will inspire Edna's independence later in the novel. Indeed, the parallels extend quite far. Like the parrot, Edna is valued by society for her physical appearance. And like the mockingbird, Mademoiselle Reisz is valued by society for her musical talent. Although the parrot and the mockingbird are different, the two birds can communicate since they share, like Edna and Mademoiselle Reisz, the common experience of confinement. The metaphor of the pet bird applies not only to Edna and Mademoiselle Reisz but also to most women in the nineteenth century. Never asked to voice their own opinions, these women were instead expected to repeat the ideas that society voiced to them through the bars of their metaphorical cages.

The tension and discord between Edna and Léonce at the beginning of the novel foreshadows the drama that will result from Edna's later departure from social conventions. Léonce does not regard his wife as a partner in marriage but as a possession. When he notices that she is sunburned from swimming, he looks at her "as one looks at a valuable piece of personal property which has suffered some damage." Soon afterward, the narrative again describes Edna from Léonce's point of view, calling her "the sole object of his existence." Léonce's perception of his wife as property was common in Louisiana society and formalized by its laws. Women were expected to be what the novel terms "mother-women," who, "fluttering about with extended, protecting wings," desired nothing more than "to efface themselves as individuals and grow wings as ministering angels." Here, the wing imagery links women to angels, but it also evokes the earlier symbolism of birds. Again, however, the narrator associates "winged" women with confinement rather than freedom. The "mother-women" have wings but are expected to use them only to protect and serve their families, not to fly. Léonce's criticism that Edna is a negligent mother reveals that in addition to feeling trapped by society, Edna is shunned by society for her deviation from its norms. Her tearful escape onto the porch prefigures later episodes in which she will similarly defy others by isolating herself from them.

The lady in black, who paces with her rosary beads, demonstrates a different sort of isolation—the patient, resigned solitude of a widow. This solitude is not the sign of independence or strength,

SUMMARY & ANALYSIS

but rather manifests a self-abnegating withdrawal from life and passion, undertaken out of utter respect for a husband's death. Throughout the novel, this black-clad woman never speaks, as if having vowed silence. Her silence contributes to her lack of individuality and her idealization within the text as the socially acceptable widow. Adèle Ratignolle exemplifies many of the same ideals as the lady in black, but she does so in the context of marriage rather than widowhood. She devotes herself solely to her husband and children, seeking nothing for herself.

And yet, notwithstanding her perfection in the roles of mother and wife, Adèle speaks with a candor that amazes Edna. Edna can hardly believe the permissiveness of Creole society in allowing everyone, including women, to discuss openly the intimacies of life such as pregnancy, undergarments, and love affairs. Men like Robert can ostentatiously play at flirting with married women, and the women can freely reciprocate.

Despite this outward appearance of liberty, however, Creole society imposes a strict code of chastity. Indeed, it is only because the rules for behavior are so rigid that a certain freedom of expression is tolerated. A Creole husband is "never jealous" because the fidelity instilled in Creole women from birth ensures that a man's possession of his wife will never be challenged.

Robert's affectionate interactions with the women of Grand Isle mimic those of the medieval practice of courtly love. Courtly love was a cultural ideal based on medieval love poetry, in which a relationship developed between a woman and a man who devoted all his actions toward her as an ideal figure. The relationship between the two lovers, however, was entirely chaste. During the middle ages, courtly love provided a woman with an opportunity—other than marriage—to express affection without losing her social respectability. Now, in nineteenth century Creole society, it seems to serve the same purpose. Yet this code of behavior strikes Edna as entirely foreign. Not a Creole herself, Edna has never been exposed to this odd balance of free speech and restrained action. She notices appreciatively that Robert never praises her with the same ambiguity he does Adèle, wavering between jest and earnestness—for she would have found such ambiguity to be confusing, she thinks, and generally "unacceptable and annoying."

Chapters VI–IX

Summary: Chapter VI

How few of us ever emerge from such beginning! How
many souls perish in its tumult!
(See Quotations, *p. 58)*

Edna cannot determine why she initially declined Robert's offer of a swim when she did wish to go with him to the beach. She begins to feel a strange light within her that shows her the way to "dreams," to "thoughtfulness," and to the "shadowy anguish" that brought her to tears the evening Léonce returned from the club. She is slowly beginning to think of herself as an individual with a relationship to the outer world, and the sound of the sea draws her soul to "inward contemplation" and wisdom that are disturbing in their newness and depth.

Summary: Chapter VII

Edna rarely discusses her feelings and private matters with others. Since childhood, she has been aware of a "dual life—the outward existence which conforms, the inward life which questions." Throughout the summer at Grand Isle, her reserve gradually erodes because of her increasingly close friendship with the candid Adèle. Walking toward the beach arm in arm, the women form a tall, stately pair. Edna, lean and mysteriously charming, wears a simple muslin and a straw hat, while Adèle, typically beautiful in the fashion of the time, protects her skin from the sun with more elaborate dress. The two women sit down on the porch of Edna's bathhouse, and Edna removes her collar and unbuttons her dress at the throat. The lady in black reads religious literature on an adjacent porch, while two lovers cuddle beneath the vacant children's tent.

Noting Edna's thoughtful silence, Adèle wants to know what Edna is thinking, and Edna searches her train of thought to reply accurately. She answers that the sea reminds her of a day when she walked through a large meadow near her childhood home in Kentucky, spreading out her arms as if swimming through the waist-high grass. Edna surmises that on that day, she had been escaping a dreary session of Sunday prayers. Although she insists that she has since adhered to religion out of a firm force of habit, Edna notes that "sometimes I feel this summer as if I were walking through the green meadow again; idly, aimlessly, unthinking and unguided."

Edna is confused when Adèle caresses her hand gently. The Creoles' open expression of affection still surprises her. Edna thinks back to the few relationships she had with other females as an adolescent. She was never close with her younger sister, Janet, and her older sister Margaret was always occupied with the household duties after their mother died. Edna's girlhood friends tended to be self-contained, much like herself, and her closest friend was a girl whose intellectual gifts Edna admired and imitated.

The relationships that most absorbed Edna were her intense, unrequited crushes on men. Her chain of infatuations was abruptly ended by her marriage to Léonce, who had courted her earnestly. She was pleased by his devotion, and when her Protestant father and sister raised objections to Léonce's Catholicism, Edna found the marriage even more appealing. But Edna also had other, more serious motivations for the marriage. Still hopelessly passionate about a well-known tragedian of the time, Edna believed that matrimony would end her unrealistic fantasies and anchor her to the conventional standards of society. Thus, she later felt a certain satisfaction in her marriage's lack of passion and excitement.

Edna's thoughts turn to her relationship with her children. She considers herself "uneven and impulsive" in her affections for them. She always feels relief when they are sent away to visit family, finding that she has "blindly assumed" the responsibilities of motherhood—responsibilities for which "[f]ate had not fitted her." She puts her head on Adèle's shoulder and finds herself expressing some of these thoughts out loud, enjoying the freshness and honesty of her own voice. Robert, followed by the two women's children, interrupts the moment of intimacy between Edna and Adèle. Edna joins the children, who have now displaced the cooing young lovers under the nearby awning, and Adèle asks Robert to walk her back to the house.

SUMMARY: CHAPTER VIII

After Edna's confession of her former passions, Adèle worries that Edna might take Robert's attentions seriously and warns him to let her alone. Insulted, he impulsively declares that he hopes Edna does take him seriously, as he is impatient with Creole women, who view him as a mere passing amusement. Adèle reminds him that if he were indeed to court married women with any seriousness, then he would ruin his reputation as a trusted gentleman. Robert begins to rationalize to Adèle the appeal of a real affair, then thinks better of it.

SUMMARY & ANALYSIS

Instead, Robert launches into stories of a well-known seducer, Alcée Arobin, until it seems Adèle has forgotten about her concern for Edna. Adèle retires to her bedroom while Robert, after a brief search for Edna on the beach, relaxes with his mother at her cottage. The two discuss the impudence of Robert's brother Victor and chat about the most recent news from Montel, Madame Lebrun's long-time suitor.

SUMMARY: CHAPTER IX
A few weeks after Adèle's conversation with Robert, Madame Lebrun and her renters hold a Saturday-night celebration to entertain their weekend guests. The party-goers request a piano duet from the fourteen-year-old Farival twins, who, formally committed by their parents at birth to become nuns, are dressed, as usual, in the blue and white colors associated with the Virgin Mary. Several other children perform, and then Adèle plays the piano while the other guests dance. Robert fetches Mademoiselle Reisz, a quarrelsome middle-aged woman, and entreats her to play for Edna.

Whenever Edna listens to Adèle practice her different pieces, images of varying emotions appear in her mind: a naked man staring out at a fleeing bird in "hopeless resignation," a dancing woman, children at play. But now, as she listens to the playing of Mademoiselle Reisz, Edna sees no pictures of these emotions. Rather, she *feels* them, and is reduced to trembling, choking tears. As Mademoiselle Reisz finishes and leaves the room, she pats Edna's shoulder and tells her that she is the only worthy listener in the entire crowd. Even so, the others have clearly enjoyed the performance. Robert suggests that the party go for a nighttime swim.

ANALYSIS: CHAPTERS VI–IX
Edna's awakening begins slowly and she seems from its beginning to expect disappointment even while she hopes for fulfillment. The dim light that first allows her to see her own latent dissatisfaction in Chapter VI is described as a "light which, showing the way, forbids it," and the suddenness with which her emotions rise to the surface renders them both disturbing and exciting. Remembering the passionate infatuations that had consumed her before marriage, Edna is suddenly struck by the contrast between those feelings and the feelings she has now in her marriage. Voicing these feelings to Adèle furthers the shedding of her outer layers of reserve, as does her sensual, almost violent reaction to the music played by Mademoiselle Reisz a few weeks later.

SUMMARY & ANALYSIS

The discrepancy between the response Adèle's piano playing evokes in Edna and that evoked by Mademoiselle Reisz speaks both to the magnitude of the older woman's talent in awakening long-dormant passions and to the magnitude of the awakening itself. Edna's jarring physical reaction to Mademoiselle Reisz's piano playing testifies to the scope of her dawning self-discovery. Similarly, the nature of her former mental images testifies to the narrowness of her earlier mindset. The piece of Adèle's that Edna had named "Solitude" conjured in Edna's mind the image of a naked man who had been left in wretched isolation by a bird. Edna associated deep emotion with a man, ignoring a woman's capacity for such experiences. The female was symbolized by the figure of the bird, with which the narrative repeatedly associates the Victorian woman. Significantly, Edna does not identify with the bird in her vision but rather with the man abandoned by it. She focused on his loneliness rather than the motivations and aims of the female figure that had left him behind. If, up until Mademoiselle Reisz's piano playing, Edna had been out of touch with the female capacity for emotion and initiative, by the end of the novel she will both recognize and realize this capacity. Her internal change will be symbolized by a refiguring of the earlier image, as Edna will emerge naked, as a feminized version of her masculine figure of solitude. The visions described in Chapter IX serve as a mark against which to measure Edna development as the novel progresses.

The secondary characters that surround Edna in these early chapters of self-discovery are quite important. They often foreshadow the later events of the narrative. The two lovers and the lady in black are conspicuously present at the beach, both before and after Edna's confessions to Adèle. They symbolize two stages in the life of a respectable Victorian woman. The lady in black, a vision of death and mourning, hovers around the innocent young lovers and serves as a constant reminder of the tragedy and isolation that are associated with love in *The Awakening*. At the celebration, the guests are entertained by the Farival twins, who were dedicated at birth to the Virgin Mary and, thus, represent the expected destiny for young Victorian girls: chaste motherhood. Like Adèle, who continues her study of music in order to brighten and beautify her home, the twins also exemplify the "artistic" woman, who was expected to use art not to express herself, but rather to be socially entertaining. In contrast, Edna will later find her own art, her painting and drawing, to be a source of great private satisfaction and pleasure.

Chapters X–XIV

Summary: Chapter X

As the crowd makes its way from the party down to the beach, Edna wonders why Robert has distanced himself from her. He no longer accompanies her constantly as he did before, although he doubles his devotion upon his return from an entire day spent away from her. It is as though he feels obligated to spend a certain number of hours with Edna.

Most of the beach-goers enter the water without a second thought, but Edna is hesitant. Despite the attempts of the other guests to teach her, she is still unable to swim. Suddenly, she feels empowered and steps into the water, earning surprised applause from her onlookers. She swims out alone, for the first time truly feeling a sense of control over her body and soul. She becomes reckless and wants to swim out "where no woman had swum before," and she scolds herself for discovering the simplicity of this act after so much time spent "splashing about like a baby!" When she looks back to the shore, however, she realizes how far she has gone and worries that she will perish from not having the strength to make it back on her own. When she arrives back on shore, she immediately dresses in the bathhouse and starts to walk home alone, despite the attempts of her husband and the other guests to retain her.

Robert runs after Edna as she makes her way home, and she asks if he thought she was afraid to walk home alone. He assures her that he knew she wasn't afraid, but he is unable to explain why he ran after her. Overwhelmed, Edna tries but fails to articulate the flood of new emotions and experiences the night has inspired in her. When Robert tells her a story of a spirit seeking a mortal worthy of visiting the semi-celestials, and of how that spirit selected Edna as his companion this night, she dismisses the tale as mere banter, not realizing that Robert is trying to express that he understands how she feels. Edna collapses into her porch hammock and Robert decides to stay with her until her husband returns. Neither speaks. The narrator comments, "No multitude of words could have been more significant than these moments of silence, or more pregnant with the first-felt throbbings of desire." When they hear the swimmers returning, Robert says good-bye and leaves.

SUMMARY: CHAPTER XI

> [Edna] perceived that her will had blazed up, stubborn
> and resistant . . . she could not realize why or how she
> should have [ever] yielded [to her husband], feeling as
> she then did.
>
> (See QUOTATIONS, p. 59)

Léonce returns and urges Edna to go to bed, but she tells him not to
wait for her—she will stay outside in the hammock. She can tell that
her stubbornness irritates him, and she realizes that up to this point
she has always submitted to her husband's requests unthinkingly,
out of habit. Edna feels so altered by her newfound defiance and
resistance that she fails to understand how she could have ever
yielded to his commands before. Léonce sits on the porch smoking
cigars and drinking wine until just before dawn. Several times he
offers wine to Edna, but each time she refuses. Sleep finally defeats
Edna's exuberant mood and forces her inside. She asks Léonce if he
is coming as well, and he replies that he will follow her once he finishes his cigar.

SUMMARY: CHAPTER XII

Edna wakes up after a few hours of restless sleep. Almost everyone
on Grand Isle is still in bed, but several people, including the two
lovers and the lady in black, are on their way to the wharf to take the
boat to the isle of *Chênière Caminada* for Sunday mass. For the first
time all summer, Edna actively requests Robert's company by asking
one of Mrs. Lebrun's servants to wake him. However, neither Edna
nor Robert thinks her request an extraordinary turn of events. They
join the other guests on the boat, and Robert speaks in Spanish to
Mariequita, a young, flirtatious Spanish girl who is brimming with
questions. Robert soon returns his attention to Edna and suggests
they explore other islands together in the upcoming days. They
laugh about the treasure they will find and then squander together.
Edna feels as though the chains that had held her to Grand Isle have
finally snapped over the course of the previous night, leaving her
unanchored and free to drift wherever she chooses.

SUMMARY: CHAPTER XIII

"How many years have I slept?" she inquired. "...A
new race of beings must have sprung up, leaving only
you and me as past relics."

(See QUOTATIONS, p. 60)

In the middle of the church service, Edna feels drowsy and troubled.
She stumbles outside, with Robert following closely behind. He
takes her to rest at the cottage of Madame Antoine, a native of the
Chênière. Once she is alone in the small bedroom, Edna removes
most of her clothing and washes up at a basin. Stretching out in bed
she observes with a new affection the firmness and fineness of her
arms, and she drifts off to sleep. When she awakens, glowing and
full of energy, she finds Robert outside in the garden, alone. She feels
as if she has slept for years and jokes that they are the only remaining
members of their race. Edna eats the dinner that Robert has pre-
pared, and when Madame Antoine returns, they rest together under
a tree, listening to the woman's stories until the sun has set and they
must return home.

SUMMARY: CHAPTER XIV

When Edna returns, Adèle reports that Edna's younger son, Etienne,
has refused to go to bed. Edna takes him on her lap and soothes him
to sleep. Her friend also tells her that Léonce was worried when
Edna did not return from the *Chênière* after mass, but once he was
assured that Edna was merely resting at Madame Antoine's and that
Madame Antoine's son would see her home, he left for the club on
business. Adèle then departs for her own cottage, hating to leave her
husband alone. After Robert and Edna put Etienne to bed, Robert
bids her good night and Edna remarks that they have been together
all day. Robert leaves, and as she awaits Léonce's return, Edna recognizes, but cannot explain, the transformation she has undergone
during her stay at Grand Isle. Because she is not tired herself, Edna
assumes that Robert isn't actually tired either, and she wonders why
he did not stay with her. She regrets his departure and sings to herself
the tune he had sung as they crossed the bay to the *Chênière*—"Ah!
Si tu savais ..." ("Ah! If only you knew").

ANALYSIS: CHAPTERS X–XIV

Edna's first swim constitutes one of the most important steps in her
process of transformation. It symbolizes her rebirth, sexual awak-

ening, and self-discovery. Edna has been unable to venture into the water because she is afraid of abandoning herself to the sea's vast and isolating expanse. After the swim, Edna has gained a new confidence in her own solitude.

When Edna descends into the water on the night of the party, she appears like a "little tottering, stumbling, clutching child, who . . . walks for the first time alone." As she gains confidence she announces to herself, "Think of the time I have lost splashing about like a baby!" Using a metaphor of rebirth and childhood growth to describe Edna's metamorphosis, Chopin's language in this passage presents Edna as a child who has just outgrown infancy and is finally a full-fledged toddler. Edna's journey is not complete, however. Although she defies societal expectations by venturing out alone, she also retains a certain childlike fear of self-reliance, as evidenced in the terror she feels when she realizes that she must depend only on herself to make it back to shore.

While Edna's achievement demonstrates her newfound wisdom and courage, the language in which the event is narrated also refers to society-wide assumptions about the helpless status of women. In many ways, Victorian law treated women like dependent minors, granting them their rights through their husbands as children would receive their rights through their fathers. At this point in her awakening, Edna's rebellious will is not paired with the fortitude required to withstand the consequences of defying social conventions, and the catastrophe of her story lies in the fact that she never quite attains this power. Thus, in addition to foreshadowing her eventual death in the ocean, the episode where she first swims also foreshadows the dangerous discrepancy between Edna's desire (her desire to swim) and her stamina (her inability to sustain the courage and strength that propel her to swim out on her own).

Edna's sense of independence and control is tested when Léonce returns to the cottage and demands that she come inside with him. Inspired by her earlier feats, Edna stands up to Léonce for the first time in six years of marriage. She even reproaches him for speaking to her with such assumed authority. Eventually, however, the pressing reality of her situation sinks in, and physical exhaustion deflates her raised spirit. As she goes inside to bed, we see the conventional structure of relations between Léonce and his wife restored. Léonce outlasts Edna's defiance and his comment that he will go to bad after he finishes his cigar proves that he can dictate his own bedtime whereas Edna, childlike, cannot.

When Edna and Robert sit on the porch in silence after she has defiantly surrendered herself to the sea, it is apparent that the event has instilled in Edna a new sexual awareness. She and Robert say nothing to one another, but, in the stillness, Edna feels "the first-felt throbbings of desire." Yet, despite their growing passion for one another, Edna and Robert are unable to relax and speak openly until they have escaped the grasp of society and convention, as the day that Edna and Robert spend together on the island of *Chênière Caminada* proves. The island, and Madame Antoine's cottage in particular, symbolizes freedom that comes from self-isolation. Only when Robert and Edna are alone, severed from reality and from their respective roles, can they express themselves and indulge in their fantasy of being together. When Edna wakes from her rest, the island seems changed. She giddily entertains the idea that all the people on Grand Isle have disappeared from earth—an idea that Robert is eager to accept. But once they return to Grand Isle, Robert leaves Edna immediately, aware that their fantasy is just that. He knows that he can no longer express his feelings with the openness their isolation on the *Chênière* afforded him. Edna, however, shows that she has not realized how forceful societal conventions are. She cannot understand why Robert refuses to stay with her upon their return to Grand Isle.

The repeated phrase of the song first sung by Robert on the boat and later by Edna—"Ah! Si tu savais"—emphasizes the dramatic irony of the plot: neither character is aware of what will come to pass. First, they have both repressed their desire for one another. The song will also come to refer to Edna's naïveté regarding the impossibility of her union with Robert. Robert's adherence to societal conventions here, despite and in contrast to Edna's own eagerness, foreshadows his similar inability to commit to her at the end of the novel.

Chapters XV–XIX

Summary: Chapter XV

One evening at dinner, several people inform Edna that Robert is leaving for Mexico that evening. Edna is shocked by this news, as she spent all morning with Robert and he mentioned nothing of his plans. The dinner conversation splits off into varied stories and questions about Mexico and its inhabitants, but Edna feels such anguish that the only time she opens her mouth is to ask Robert what time he will leave. After finishing her coffee, Edna promptly retires to her cottage, where she occupies herself with housework and the needs of her sons. Mrs. Lebrun sends a message requesting that Edna sit with her until Robert leaves, but Edna replies that she doesn't feel well and wants to stay in. Adèle comes down to check on Edna and agrees that Robert's abrupt departure seems unfair and unkind. Unable to persuade Edna to accompany her back to the main house, Adèle departs unaccompanied to rejoin the others' conversation. Robert himself then visits Edna. He bids her good-bye and is unable to say when he will return. She expresses her disappointment and offense at his spontaneous and unannounced departure, but he stops short of giving her a full explanation, fearing that he will reveal his true feelings for her. Edna asks Robert to write her and is bothered by Robert's uncharacteristic, distant reply: "I will, thank you. Good-by." Edna broods in the darkness and tries to prevent herself from crying, recognizing in her relations with Robert the same symptoms of infatuation she knew as a youth.

Summary: Chapter XVI

Edna is constantly possessed by thoughts of Robert. She feels as though her entire existence has been dulled by his departure. She often visits Madame Lebrun to chat and study the pictures of Robert in the family albums. Edna reads the letter Robert sent to his mother before departing for Mexico from New Orleans and feels a momentary pang of jealousy that he did not write to her instead.

Everyone finds it natural that Edna misses Robert, even her husband. When Edna learns that Léonce saw Robert in New Orleans before his departure for Mexico, she questions him extensively about their meeting. Edna sees no harm in this interrogation, for her feelings for Robert are nothing like her feelings for her husband. She is used to keeping her emotions and thoughts to herself. Edna had once tried to express this ownership of emotions to Adèle, telling her: "I would give up the unessential; I would give my money, I would give my life for my children, but I wouldn't give myself." Adèle cannot understand what more one could do for her children than give up her life.

Shortly before the summer's end, Mademoiselle Reisz approaches Edna on the beach, curious about the effect of Robert's absence on Edna. A conversation ensues in which Mademoiselle tells Edna that Madame Lebrun is partial to her other son Victor, despite Victor's impudence. The two brothers apparently have a history of squabbles. Mademoiselle Reisz does not realize that she has upset Edna, and she gives Edna her address in New Orleans, urging her to visit.

Summary: Chapter XVII

Léonce takes great pride in his possessions and enjoys walking around his lavishly decorated New Orleans home and examining his household goods. Every Tuesday for the past six years Edna has observed her reception day—a day set aside each week for receiving visitors—dressing handsomely and not leaving the house. A few weeks after returning to New Orleans, she and Léonce sit down to dinner, Edna wearing an ordinary housedress rather than her usual Tuesday gown. Léonce notices her attire and asks about Edna's day. She replies that she was not at home to receive visitors, nor did she leave the servants with an excuse with which they might placate her guests. Léonce is angry with her, fearing that her neglect of her social duties will jeopardize his business relations with the husbands of her visitors. Complaining that the cook has produced a substandard meal, Léonce leaves mid-meal to take dinner at the club, a practice to which Edna has become accustomed over the past several weeks. After finishing her meal, Edna goes to her room, pacing while she tears her thin handkerchief into pieces. She throws her wedding ring to the floor and tries unsuccessfully to crush it. Feeling the need to destroy something, she shatters a glass vase on the hearth.

Summary: Chapter XVIII

The next morning Edna declines Léonce's request that she meet him in town and instead tries to work on some sketches. Not in the mood for sketching, however, she decides to visit Adèle, whom she finds at home folding newly laundered clothing. Edna informs her friend that she wants to take drawing lessons and presents her portfolio, seeking praise and encouragement in the matter. Edna gives some sketches to Adèle and stays for dinner. Upon leaving, Edna realizes with a strong sense of depression that the perfect domestic harmony enjoyed by the Ratignolles is entirely undesirable to her. She pities Adèle's "colorless existence" and "blind contentment."

Summary: Chapter XIX

Edna has entirely abandoned the practice of staying home to receive callers on Tuesdays. Léonce, severely displeased by Edna's refusal to submit to his demands, scolds his wife for spending her days painting instead of caring for the "comfort of her family." He bids her think of Adèle, who never allows her love of music to distract her from her household responsibilities. Léonce sometimes speculates that Edna suffers from some mental disturbance, and he leaves Edna alone to paint and sing Robert's song to herself as she dreams of the sea and Grand Isle. Her daily moods fluctuate wildly between inexplicable joy and equally intense sorrow.

ANALYSIS: CHAPTERS XV–XIX

The odd farewell between Edna and Robert demonstrates their contrasting attitudes toward upholding the rules assigned by society and tradition. Robert never addresses Edna directly by her first name, saying simply, "Good-by, my dear Mrs. Pontellier." He seems consumed by the idea that Léonce already has the rights of possession over Edna, and Robert's use of the words "*my dear*" is his only expression of his feelings for Edna. Edna, on the other hand, calls Robert directly by his first name, clinging to his hand as she asks, "Write to me when you get there, won't you, Robert?" Robert, who has recognized the chemistry between himself and Edna since the first days of their acquaintance, is able to overlook his feelings for Edna when etiquette requires. She, on the other hand, has not yet reached either stage. It is only as Robert walks away that she recognizes the symptoms of youthful infatuation in her feelings for him.

Edna's sexual awakening in her relations with Robert is intimately connected to her other dawning awarenesses. As she has begun to recognize and listen to her own emotions, she has come to feel an entitlement to them. Thus, she does not feel remorse at inciting Léonce to talk about Robert, nor does she keep from Adèle her unwillingness to give up herself for her children. While her farewell with Robert is revelatory of the still-undeveloped nature of Edna's sexual awareness, her awakening has already progressed quite far on a more general level. Edna, unlike Adèle, can see that there is something more valuable than one's life, that there is a reality more profound and important than physical existence.

After returning to New Orleans, Edna begins to allow this inner life to emerge and expand to the point that it affects those around her. She occupies her time with painting rather than domestic chores and is consumed by her own moods. Léonce's reactions do not prove him to be any less self-centered, however. When he notices her neglect of household chores, he is worried about the negative effect Edna's actions may have on his social standing rather than her unhappiness. His absorption with respectability and appearance, which prevents Léonce from gaining any insight into his wife's true nature, is also evident in the pleasure he derives from the lavish goods that furnish his home. His lack of insight emerges when he wonders whether Edna is going mad because she is behaving quite unlike herself. In fact, the text tells us, Edna is "becoming herself" and "daily casting aside that fictitious self which we assume like a garment with which to appear to the world."

Keeping this remark in mind, literal garments gather increasing importance in these chapters as Edna expresses her rebellion in part through her clothing. Upset by the news of Robert's departure, Edna strips down to her dressing gown. The layers she removes could be seen to symbolize Victorian discretion, stripped away by her growing sexual awareness. And, back in New Orleans, Edna's disregard for the traditional Tuesday reception is revealed to Léonce by the ordinary housedress she wears in place of her reception gown. The restriction and theatricality of social customs are embodied in the restrictive costuming that accompanies those customs.

Chapters XX–XXIV

Summary: Chapter XX
During one of her spells of depression, Edna decides to pay Mademoiselle Reisz a visit in order to listen to her play the piano. Finding that the woman has moved, Edna visits Madame Lebrun in search of Mademoiselle Reisz's new address. Robert's brother Victor answers the door and sends the servant to fetch his mother. He launches into a story about his exploits of the previous evening, which Edna cannot help finding entertaining. Madame Lebrun appears, complaining of how few visitors she receives, and Victor tells Edna the contents of Robert's two letters from Mexico. Edna is depressed to hear that Robert enclosed no message for her. She asks about Mademoiselle Reisz, and Madame Lebrun gives her the pianist's new address. Victor then escorts Edna outside. After Edna leaves, the Lebruns comment to each other on Edna's ravishing appearance, and Victor notes, "Some way she doesn't seem like the same woman."

Summary: Chapter XXI
Mademoiselle Reisz laughs with happiness and surprise when Edna arrives at her door. Edna's frank admission that she is unsure of whether she likes Mademoiselle pleases her host. Mademoiselle

mentions nonchalantly that Robert has sent her a letter from Mexico, in which he has written almost entirely about Edna. Edna's plea to read the letter is denied, although Mademoiselle mentions that Robert requested she play for Edna "that Impromptu of Chopin's." Edna continues to beg Mademoiselle to play the piano and to allow her to read Robert's letter.

Mademoiselle Reisz asks Edna what she has been doing with her time and is surprised to hear of Edna's current desire to become an artist. She warns her that an artist must be brave, possessing "a courageous soul . . . that dares and defies." Edna assures her that she has persistence if nothing else, and Mademoiselle Reisz laughs, gives Edna the letter, and begins to play the Chopin Impromptu that Edna requested. The music deeply affects Edna, and she weeps as the pianist glides between the Impromptu and another piece, "Isolde's song." When Edna asks if she may visit again, Mademoiselle Reisz replies that she is welcome at all times.

SUMMARY: CHAPTER XXII

Léonce expresses his concern about Edna to Doctor Mandelet, his friend and the family's physician. Léonce confides that he and his wife are no longer sleeping together, noting, "She's got some sort of notion in her head concerning the eternal rights of women." The doctor asks if Edna has been associating with a circle of "pseudo-intellectual women," alluding to the contemporary women's clubs that served to educate their members and to organize them politically. Léonce replies that Edna no longer seems to see anyone at all. She mopes around the house, wanders the streets alone, and has abandoned even her Tuesday receptions.

Having ruled out Edna's female companions as the source of her estrangement, Dr. Mandelet inquires about Edna's heredity. Léonce assures the doctor that Edna descends from a respectable Presbyterian family, but he admits that her younger sister Janet, who is about to be married, "is something of a vixen." Doctor Mandelet suggests that Léonce send Edna to the wedding so that she can be with her family, but Léonce replies that Edna has already declared her unwillingness to attend. She told her husband, "a wedding is one of the most lamentable spectacles on earth." After a pause, the doctor assures Léonce that this "passing whim" will run its course if he lets her alone for awhile, even allowing her to stay home alone when he leaves on business if that is what she wishes. Doctor Mandelet promises to attend dinner at the Pontellier home in order to study

Edna inconspicuously. Despite the doctor's suspicion that Edna may have another man in her life, the doctor takes his leave without making any inquiries along that line.

SUMMARY: CHAPTER XXIII

Edna's father, a former colonel in the Confederate army, stays for a few days in New Orleans to select a wedding gift for Janet and to purchase a suit for the wedding. Edna is not very close with the Colonel, who retains a certain military air from his war days. Nevertheless, the two are companionable, and Edna decides to sketch her father in her studio. The Colonel takes Edna's painting very seriously, posing patiently for her sketches. She takes him to Adèle's *soirée musicale* (an evening of musical entertainment), where Adèle enchants him by being flirtatious and flattering. As usual, Léonce refuses to attend Adèle's gathering, preferring the diversion of the club. Adèle disapproves of Léonce's club and remarks to Edna that the couple should spend more time together at home in the evenings, an idea Edna rebuffs by asserting that they "wouldn't have anything to say to each other."

Edna takes delight in serving her father hand and foot, appreciating their companionship but realizing that her interest in him will likely fade. Doctor Mandelet comes to dinner at the Pontellier home but notices nothing in Edna's behavior to arouse concern. She seems to him positively radiant as she relates her day at the races with her father and describes the charming people they met there. Everyone takes turns telling stories for entertainment: the Colonel speaks of war times, Léonce recalls memories from his youth, and the doctor tells a tale of a female patient who eventually came to her senses after pursuing multiple stray affections. Edna responds to this with a fictional story of a woman who disappears forever into the islands with her lover. Edna pretends to have heard the tale from Madame Antoine, and the doctor is the only person who perceives the implications of Edna's tale. On his way home, he muses, "I hope to heaven it isn't Alcée Arobin."

SUMMARY: CHAPTER XXIV

Edna and the Colonel engage in a heated argument over Edna's refusal to attend Janet's wedding in New York, but Léonce doesn't intervene, resolving instead to attend the wedding himself in order to deflect the insult of Edna's absence. The Colonel criticizes Léonce's lack of control over Edna, maintaining that a man must use "authority" and "coercion" in all matters concerning his wife. As

Léonce's departure for New York approaches, Edna becomes suddenly attentive to and affectionate with Léonce, remembering his many kindnesses and even shedding a few tears when the day of his departure arrives. The children, too, are leaving for a while, to spend some time with Léonce's mother, Madame Pontellier, who requested their company at her home in the country. Once alone, Edna is overtaken with a "radiant peace." She surveys her house and gardens as if for the first time, dines alone in her nightgown, and reads in the library every night before bed.

ANALYSIS: CHAPTERS XX–XXIV

The contrast between Edna and Adèle grows increasingly apparent in these chapters, as Edna drifts ever farther from the ideal "mother-woman" embodied by Adèle. Edna is increasingly preoccupied with the idea of abandoning her former lifestyle for a career in painting, whereas Adèle sees no difference between Edna's art and her own music, which she uses, not as an outlet for her emotions, but as a way to serve and nurture her domestic and social relations. Adèle's *soirée musicale* exemplifies her use of music as a social tool.

In Chapter XVIII, Edna was bothered by Adèle's subservience to her husband's opinion. When he spoke at dinner, Adèle gave him her complete attention, even to the point of laying down her fork to hear him better. Edna is wholly uninterested in experiencing for herself the union that Adèle and her husband share, and she thinks that they cannot fully appreciate life beyond the narrow confines of convention. When she saw Adèle's behavior in Chapter XVIII, she thought to herself that "the taste of life's delirium" is preferable to the "blind contentment" of the Ratignolles. In Chapter XXIII, Edna again finds her friend's behavior distasteful. When Edna takes her father to one of Adèle's musical soirées, Adèle plays the perfect hostess, flirting with glances, gestures, and compliments. Edna looks down upon such coquetry, and although she enjoys being noticed by the men, she waits for them to approach her during lulls in the music. Edna's attitude reveals her desire to engage with men on a more equal and less self-degrading manner.

While Edna finds herself feeling distanced from her former confidante Adèle, she becomes increasingly close to Mademoiselle Reisz, whom she is beginning to resemble. An inspiration to Edna's awakening, Mademoiselle Reisz is a self-sufficient and independent woman. She is passionate about her music and ignores the opinions of those around her. Through her relationship with the pianist,

Edna becomes more aware of herself as a woman capable of passionate art *and* passionate love. While the two capacities are interconnected, Mademoiselle Reisz serves to further each specifically. Not only is the pianist in touch with her own artistic emotions, she is, on a more pragmatic level, in touch with the traveling Robert, and she is the only one to whom he speaks about his love for Edna.

After playing Edna's requested piece, the Chopin Impromptu, Mademoiselle Reisz takes up a song from Wagner's opera *Tristan and Isolde.* The opera tells the tragic love story of two characters who resemble Edna and Robert: a married woman and a single man who can be together only in death. In the piece the mademoiselle plays, Isolde pledges her decision to follow Tristan in death. Although the text does not quote the words Isolde sings here, an acquaintance with the lyrics allows the reader to access a bit of discreet but poignant foreshadowing. Isolde sings: "As they swell and roar around me, shall I breathe them, shall I listen to them? Shall I sip them, plunge beneath them, to expire in sweet perfume? In the surging swell, in the ringing sound, in the vast wave of the world's breath—to drown, to sink, unconscious—supreme bliss." Isolde's words prefigure Edna's final, suicidal, entry into the ocean waves.

Léonce, blinded by conventional views of women's behavior, sees Edna's newfound independence as a sign of mental illness. Doctor Mandelet shows more insight by advising Léonce to allow Edna to do as she wishes. Doctor Mandelet intends his tale at dinner to be both a diagnostic tool and a subtle admonition to Edna, and Edna shows that she understands the Doctor's meaning by countering with her own elaborately detailed and captivating tale of a woman who escapes with her lover and never returns. Only the doctor, Edna, and the reader are able to discern the meaningful subtext that is present in these dinner table stories.

CHAPTERS XXV–XXIX

SUMMARY: CHAPTER XXV

The initial restfulness and ease Edna feels after the departure of her family quickly dissipates. At times, Edna is optimistic about her future and places her trust in the promise of youth. On other days, she stays indoors and broods, feeling that life is passing her by. On days when she is feeling sociable, Edna visits the friends she made at Grand Isle or goes to the races. One day, Alcée Arobin and Mrs. Highcamp, whom Edna had run into recently while at the races with her father, call on her to accompany them to the track. Alcée had met Edna before, but on the day he ran into Edna with her father, Alcée found Edna's knowledge of racehorses exciting and magnetic and became enamored with her. Alcée escorts Edna home after dinner with the Highcamps, persuading her to attend the races with him again. Edna is restless after he leaves and regrets not having asked him to stay for a while. She sleeps restlessly, waking in the middle of the night, and, remembering that she has forgotten to write her regular letter to Léonce, begins to compose in her head the words she will write him the next day.

A few days later Alcée and Edna attend the races alone. Alcée behaves as he is known to with attractive young women—without inhibition. He stays for dinner with Edna after the races and discovers, through casual conversation and interaction, the sexuality latent within her. His boldness makes Edna nervous, for, despite her attraction to Alcée, she feels that she is being led toward an act of infidelity. She firmly sends Alcée away and, when alone again, stares at the hand he has kissed, feeling as though she has been somehow unchaste. It is not her husband whom she fears she has betrayed, however: her thoughts are of Robert only.

Summary: Chapter XXVI

Alcée writes Edna an elaborate letter of apology. She is embarrassed that she took him so seriously before, and she responds with light banter. Alcée takes Edna's response as a license for further flirtation and soon resumes a level of familiarity that first astonishes Edna and then pleases her, as it appeals to her animalistic sexual urges.

Edna continues to visit Mademoiselle Reisz, who is helpful at times of emotional turmoil. During one visit, Edna announces that she is moving out of her house because she has grown tired of looking after it and feels no real connection to it as her own. She plans to rent a small house around the corner, which she will pay for with her winnings from the racetrack and the profits from her sketches. Mademoiselle Reisz knows that Edna's motivation to move is more complicated than she claims. She gets Edna to admit that she wants to move to the smaller house because it will enable her to be independent and free. Yet even after this confession, neither Mademoiselle Reisz nor Edna herself can explain completely the reason for Edna's sudden decision.

As usual, Mademoiselle Reisz gives Edna Robert's latest letter. She does not tell Robert that Edna sees his letters because Robert is trying to forget the woman whom he recognizes is "not free to listen to him or belong to him." Edna is shocked to read that Robert will soon be returning to New Orleans. During the heated discussion that follows, Mademoiselle Reisz tests Edna's devotion to Robert by making false claims about the nature of love. She ultimately realizes that Edna's feelings are pure and laughs at the way Edna blushes when she finally confesses aloud her love for Robert. Edna returns home full of excitement. She sends bonbons to her sons and writes Léonce a cheerful letter in which she states her intent to move into the smaller house.

Summary: Chapter XXVII

Later that evening, Alcée finds Edna in fine although contemplative spirits. She notes to him that she sometimes feels "devilishly wicked" by conventional standards but cannot think of herself that way. Alcée caresses Edna's face and listens to her talk about her visit to Mademoiselle Reisz earlier in the day. Mademoiselle Reisz placed her hand on Edna's shoulder blades and warned her that the bird that attempts to fly above tradition and prejudice must have strong wings, or it will "fall back to earth, battered and bruised." Alcée asks Edna where she will fly, and she replies that she is not contemplating any "extraordinary flights." In fact, Edna claims, she only "half comprehend[s]" the older woman. Alcée kisses Edna, and she responds by "clasping his head." Alcée's kiss is "the first . . . of her life to which her nature had really responded. It was a flaming torch that kindled desire."

Summary: Chapter XXVIII

After Alcée leaves, Edna weeps. She feels guilty when she considers the material possessions surrounding her, all of which her husband has provided. She understands the irresponsible nature of her actions, yet she feels no shame or regret. Instead, it is the thought of Robert and of her love for him, growing ever "quicker, fiercer" and "more overpowering," that affects her. She suddenly feels that she at last understands the world around her, "as if a mist had been lifted from her eyes, enabling her to look upon and comprehend the significance of life. . . ." Her only regret is that her kiss with Alcée was not motivated by love.

Summary: Chapter XXIX

Without waiting for Léonce's reply to her letter, Edna prepares to move to the house around the block, which one of Edna's servants dubs the "pigeon house," likening it in size and appearance to the dovecotes in which the upper classes would keep domesticated pigeons for show or sport. When Alcée arrives, he finds Edna dressed in an old dress and kerchief, packing only the possessions that Léonce did not buy for her. She is neither rude to her friend nor is she particularly attentive. Rather, Edna is totally absorbed in her work. Alcée reminds her of the dinner celebration she had planned, and she tells him it is set for the night before her move. He begs to see her sooner, and she scolds him but laughs as she does so, looking at him "with eyes that at once gave him the courage to wait and made it torture to wait."

ANALYSIS: CHAPTERS XXV–XXIX

Edna's rebellion involves her need to satisfy her physical as well as artistic desires. Alcée presents an outlet for her animalism, which gains strength as the two spend more and more time together, until finally Edna finds she can longer fight against it. When Alcée first presses his lips to Edna's hand, she attempts to impress upon him her fidelity and disinterest. While her eyes still display her "old, vanishing self," the sexual desires within Edna are pressing on her from the inside, seeking expression. Edna finally succumbs to Alcée's seductions after she confesses to Mademoiselle Reisz—aloud for the first time—her love for Robert. It may seem ironic that she gives herself to one man just after declaring her devotion to another, but, in terms of Edna's development, the two acts are joined. Both are part of the same process of passionate release: Edna's verbal admission to love in one corner of her life gives her the strength to pursue it further in another.

During her conversation with Alcée, Edna directly voices her desire for self-realization. She wants to become more acquainted with herself, but she cannot do so within the constraints of social conventions. By those standards, she is "wicked"—subverting order, descending into selfishness and hedonism—yet she herself cannot interpret her desire for an independent identity as a "wicked" endeavor. Alcée becomes peevish at her philosophical tarrying; he wants her to play the role of the typical, infatuated adulteress. Clearly, Alcée is used to having the upper hand in his romantic relationships and views women as pleasurable conquests.

Edna refuses to be treated or behave as a stereotype. In her growing independence, she has declared that she will never again be the possession of another, and she abides by this statement in her affair with Alcée. She expects him to make allowances for her own needs.

When Alcée finds her in a frenzy of preparation for her move, Edna will not agree to see him at his convenience. Moreover, he does not find her "languishing, reproachful, or indulging in sentimental tears" as he most likely expected. Edna is unwilling to let her affair, the first sexual relationship she has had that is not one of possession, consume her life. Her relationship with Alcée does not keep her from pursuing any other aspects of her awakening. It simply quells the sexual desire that had consumed her days, and even her dreams.

Edna's move to the "pigeon house" also allows her to move away from her husband's possessive hold over her. Edna no longer has to look at the material objects that Léonce has purchased, and which remind her of his ownership of her. The objects have also served as a sort of reproach to Edna, making her feel guilty for her infidelity toward the man who has provided her with her livelihood. Once distanced from these reminders and alone in a new space of her own, Edna can enjoy a temporary escape from convention. She can behave as she likes, without regard to how others will view her actions. Moreover, she believes the move may constitute a first, practical step in consummating her relationship with Robert. Knowing that Robert has gone to Mexico in order to avoid having an affair with a woman who is already the possession of another man, Edna believes that by freeing herself of the financial chains that bind her to Léonce, she can clear the path for a relationship with the man she loves.

The house's nickname foreshadows Edna's tragic fate. While it does provide Edna with independence and isolation, allowing her to progress in her sexual awakening and to throw off Léonce's authority, Edna will soon find that it offers less liberty than it initially seemed to promise. Edna escapes the gilded cage that Léonce's house constituted, but she confines herself within a new sort of cage. Social convention—and Robert's concession to it—continues to keep Edna trapped and domesticated. Indeed, not only may Edna's move have failed to improve her lot, the text's symbolism suggests that the change of house may threaten actual damage to the vibrancy of her spirit. Whereas Edna was initially associated, in Chapter I, with a brightly colored and multilingual caged parrot, she is now likened to a dull gray pigeon, a comparatively languid and inarticulate creature.

Mademoiselle Reisz recognizes in Edna the same desire for escape and independence with which she has lived her own life. Knowing the hardships that Edna will face in her struggle to live outside convention, the older woman warns her protégé of the strength she will need, much in the same manner of her earlier advice on the "brave" and "courageous" artistic soul. Mademoiselle Reisz's counsel about the bird fluttering back to earth continues the novel's extended metaphorical association of Edna to a bird. It is also an obvious foreshadowing of Edna's death; the image returns just before Edna's suicide.

Chapters XXX–XXXV

Summary: Chapter XXX

The dinner Edna hosts in celebration of her new home is small and exclusive. Her guests include high-society friends from the racetrack, as well as Mademoiselle Reisz, Victor Lebrun, and, of course, Alcée. Adèle, who is unable to come because she is nearing the end of her pregnancy, sends her husband in her place. Edna has decorated the table and surroundings decadently, and the entire room shimmers with gold and yellow accents. She announces that it is her twenty-ninth birthday and proposes that the party drink to her health with a cocktail invented by the Colonel to commemorate Janet's wedding. Alcée proposes that they drink to the Colonel's health instead, to celebrate "the daughter he invented." In her magnificent gown, Edna seems a woman who "rules, who looks on, who stands alone." However, she is inwardly overtaken with longing and hopelessness, her thoughts fixated on Robert.

Mademoiselle Reisz and Adèle's husband take their leave and the remaining guests turn their attention to Victor, whom Mrs. Highcamp has decorated with a garland of roses and a silken scarf, which turn him into "a vision of Oriental beauty." Someone begs Victor to sing and he accepts dramatically, looking at Edna and beginning, "Ah! Si tu savais!" Edna orders him to stop, slamming her glass down so heavily that she breaks it. Victor, however, continues, until Edna clasps her hand over his mouth and repeats her demand. He agrees, kissing her hand with a "pleasing sting," and the guests sense that the night has come to a close.

Summary: Chapter XXXI

Alcée stays with Edna after everyone has left and assists her as she shuts up the big house. He accompanies her to the pigeon house, which he has filled with flowers as a surprise. He tells her he will leave, but when he feels her beginning to respond to his caresses his sits beside her and covers her shoulders with kisses until she becomes "supple to his gentle, seductive entreaties."

SUMMARY: CHAPTER XXXII

> *The pigeon-house pleased her ... There was ... a feeling of having descended in the social scale, with a corresponding sense of having risen in the spiritual.*
> *(See* QUOTATIONS, *p. 61)*

Léonce writes a letter of stern disapproval in response to Edna's move. He does not question her motives but worries that people will think he is suffering financial difficulties. To avert these suspicions, he arranges to have his home remodeled by a respected architect. In a newspaper, he advertises his intention to take a vacation abroad with Edna while the remodeling is under way. In her husband's continued absence, Edna feels her sense of individuality and spirituality growing. She visits her children at their grandmother's country home in Iberville and enjoys herself so much that she continues to think of their voices and excitement throughout her trip back to New Orleans.

SUMMARY: CHAPTER XXXIII

Adèle pays Edna a visit. She inquires about the dinner party, inspects her friend's new home, and complains that Edna has neglected her. She confesses to Edna that she worries about the impulsive and reckless nature of her actions, adding that perhaps she should not be living alone in the little house. As she leaves, she warns Edna to be careful of her reputation, as there is gossip about Alcée's visits and "his attentions alone are . . . enough to ruin a woman's name." After a stream of callers interrupts Edna's painting, she decides to visit Mademoiselle Reisz. The pianist is not at home, however, so Edna enters the apartment to wait for her. She hears a knock at the door and gasps in surprise when she sees the caller is Robert, who has been back in town for two days. Edna begins to doubt his love, wondering why he hadn't come to see her immediately. Robert's speech is rushed and embarrassed; only during a brief pause do his eyes reveal to Edna the same tenderness she had seen on Grand Isle. She asks why he broke his promise to write her, and he replies that he never supposed his letters would interest her. Edna says that she doesn't believe his excuse, and she decides that she will not wait any longer for Mademoiselle Reisz's return.

Robert walks Edna home, and she invites him in for dinner at the pigeon house. She revels in the thought that her dreams are now coming true. At first Robert declines her offer, but, when he sees the disappointment and pain in Edna's face, he soon consents. Inside, Robert discovers a photograph of Alcée that Edna claims she has kept as a study for a sketch. His repeated questions about the photograph manifest his suspicions and Edna quickly changes the subject to Robert's experiences in Mexico. He tells her that he worked machine-like the whole time, devoting his thoughts solely to the time he spent with Edna on Grand Isle and the *Chênière*. When he asks about her own experiences in New Orleans, she echoes his nostalgic words almost verbatim. He tells her, "Mrs. Pontellier, you are cruel." They remain in silence until dinner is announced.

Summary: Chapter XXXIV

During dinner, Edna and Robert lose their earlier honesty and vivacity and become stiff and ceremonious. After they have eaten, they sit in the parlor, and Edna questions Robert about the young Mexican girl whose gift of a tobacco pouch has become the topic of discussion. Alcée drops by with a message for Edna about a card party. As soon as he sees Robert, Alcée begins to talk about the seductive beauty of Mexican girls. Robert is on edge and answers somewhat coldly. Soon afterward, he takes his leave of Edna, who remains with Alcée. Alcée asks Edna to go out for a nighttime drive but she sends him away, preferring to be alone. For the rest of the evening she thinks over her encounter with Robert, feeling suddenly distant from him and moved by pangs of jealousy as she imagines him with a beautiful young Mexican girl.

Summary: Chapter XXXV

The next morning Edna awakes with hope, convinced that she has overreacted to what she perceived as Robert's reserve of the night before. She tells herself that she will undoubtedly receive a visit from him that afternoon or evening. At breakfast, she reads letters from Raoul and from Léonce, who indicates his plans to return in March to take her on a journey abroad. Alcée has also sent a note, declaring his devotion and his trust that, however faintly, Edna returns his affection. She writes back cheerfully to her children and puts Alcée's note under the maid's stove-lid, choosing not to respond. Her response to Léonce's letter about the proposed trip is evasive. Edna does not intend to mislead her husband, but she is unable to conceive of the vacation or, for that matter, of reality, because "she had abandoned herself to Fate and awaited the consequences with indifference."

Days pass without a visit from Robert. Edna does not wish to visit Mademoiselle Reisz or Madame Lebrun because she fears that they may think she is eager to seek out Robert's company. She awakes each morning in a state of hope and expectation, but retires each evening in despair. One night, she accepts Alcée's invitation to accompany him out to the lake; afterward they return to her home, slipping into the physical intimacy that has become more and more frequent between them. Lying in bed that night, Edna feels freed of despondency, yet the next day she fails to feel the sense of hope that has greeted her on the past several mornings.

ANALYSIS: CHAPTERS XXX–XXXV

Although Edna does not miss the duties and limitations of her past, she has begun to feel the isolation of her current lifestyle. Her isolation is alleviated only by lust, not by the more genuine, purer kind of emotion she shares with her sons. Her visit to Iberville reveals that Edna still feels a sense of responsibility to her children, despite her feeling that she is no longer bound by matrimonial duty. Whereas Edna resented her obligation to her husband, her responsibility to her sons is pleasing. Edna's unhappiness about leaving her children suggests a developing, although still unconscious, understanding of the effect her infidelities will have on the lives of her boys. Consciously, however, Edna thinks only of Robert's return, dwelling on the idealized version of true love that she believes awaits them.

When Robert does return, the romantic, dreamlike reunion that Edna had imagined is replaced by an uncomfortable sense of tension. As they walk past her former home on the way to the pigeon house, Robert remarks, "I never knew you in your home." Edna's glib reply—"I am glad you did not"—reveals her unrealistic expectations for their relationship. She simplistically assumes that her new home and new independence will foster a love untainted by her past life, and she believes that Robert will be able to see her only as she is now, untethered from her prior identity. But Robert's behavior shows that he does not believe the past can be so easily laid aside and forgotten. He continues to call Edna by her married name, he mentions Léonce several times, and he refers to the Pontellier mansion as Edna's "home," not as her former home. The lovers' contrasting attitudes toward Edna's past foreshadow the opposing decisions the two will make at the end of the novel, when faced with the prospect of honoring their emotions only by way of adultery.

The photograph of Alcée mars Edna and Robert's evening alone on at least two different levels. As a suggestion of a third presence, it shatters their temporary illusion of being a world unto themselves. It also may serve to subtly weaken the bond they share by lowering Edna in Robert's esteem. Although the text does not state whether Robert knows about Edna's affair with Alcée, it is clear that he is aware of Alcée's reputation. He is shocked when his discovers Alcée's photograph in Edna's home, and in Chapter VIII he tells a disapproving story about Alcée to Edna and Adèle on Grand Isle. Robert may have begun to wonder whether Edna is easily seduced.

Robert reacts to Alcée's arrival at the pigeon house after dinner as he reacted to her photograph. As if yielding to Alcée's higher authority, Robert leaves Edna immediately. Alcée's later comments indicate that he had been unaware of Edna's acquaintance with Robert, which renders ironically accurate Alcée's unknowing comment, "I am always less fortunate than Robert. Has he been imparting tender confidences?" Edna will have nothing to do with her lover because she is too consumed by thoughts of her confusing reunion.

Since they first met, Edna and Robert have been misunderstanding one another with increasing severity. On Grand Isle, they understood each other and the time they spent together was harmonious. Since Robert left for Mexico, he has not communicated with Edna at all. She learned of his feelings indirectly, by reading his letters to Mademoiselle Reisz. Now, their renewed relationship is fraught, for the first time, with miscommunication. When Edna echoes almost verbatim Robert's expression of his nostalgia and misery during their time apart, he misunderstands her mimicry of his statement to be a form of mockery and consequently declares her "cruel." And, although Robert stays away from Edna because he recognizes the impossibility of their union, Edna doesn't understand his distance and soon returns to her former depression and hopelessness.

Thus, when she sees Alcée again, she is so consumed by her unrequited passion for Robert that Alcée's touch provides the only possibility for peace, however fleeting. Robert is now much nearer at hand than he has been for the past months, but she turns to Alcée for lustful satisfaction. In doing so, Edna is for the first time utterly honest about her sexual needs. She finally admits to herself that her affair with Alcée has not been solely in anticipation of Robert's return but also in response to the sheer, anarchic passions raging within her, independent of any emotional devotion. Her forthright acknowledgment of her desire marks the completion of her sexual awakening.

Chapters XXXVI–XXXIX

Summary: Chapter XXXVI

One day Edna bumps into Robert in her favorite garden café, which is nestled in the suburbs of New Orleans. Robert reacts with uneasiness and surprise at the unexpected encounter but consents to stay and dine with Edna. Although Edna had decided to act with reserve if she were to see Robert, she cannot help but be plain and honest with him. She expresses her disappointment at his own seeming indifference, telling him he is selfish and inconsiderate of her emotions. She emphasizes that she is not afraid to share her opinions, however "unwomanly" he may think them. He responds by accusing her of cruelty, of wishing him to "bare a wound for the pleasure of looking at it, without the intention or power of healing it." Retreating from his display of anger, Edna returns to pleasantries and thoughtless banter.

The two go to the pigeon house, arriving after dark. When she returns to the room after leaving to wash up, Edna leans over Robert as he sits in a chair, and kisses him. In response, he takes her into his arms and holds her, kissing her back. He confesses that his trip to Mexico was an attempt to escape his love for her. In Mexico, he says, he fantasized that she could become his wife, that perhaps Léonce would "set her free." Edna declares that the fantasy is reality, because she is no longer one of Léonce's possessions and will give herself to whomever she pleases. Robert is shocked, perhaps even dismayed, by her announcement.

Edna's servant interrupts to tell Edna that Adèle is in labor and wants Edna to be with her. Edna leaves, assuring Robert that she loves only him and that they shall soon "be everything to each other." He begs her to stay, able to think only of holding and keeping her, but she tells him to wait because she will return.

Summary: Chapter XXXVII

Adèle is irritable and exhausted as she awaits the arrival of the doctor. Edna begins to feel uneasy as memories of her own childbirth experiences surface but seem removed, vague, and undefined. Although she stays by her friend's side, she desperately wants to leave. She watches the scene of "torture" with a feeling of "inward agony" and a "flaming, outspoken revolt against the ways of Nature." When the ordeal is over, Edna kisses Adèle good-bye, as Adèle whispers earnestly, "Think of the children, Edna. Oh think of the children!"

SUMMARY: CHAPTER XXXVIII

> *"Perhaps it is better to wake up after all, even to suffer, rather than to remain a dupe to illusions all one's life."*
> *(See* QUOTATIONS, *p. 62)*

Doctor Mandelet, who is also Adèle's doctor, walks Edna to the pigeon house. He voices his concern that another, less impressionable, woman ought to have stayed with Adèle. He asks Edna if she will go abroad with Léonce, and Edna replies that she will not and that she refuses to be forced into anything anymore. She begins to say that no one has any right to oblige her to do what she does not wish, excepting, perhaps, children. Although Edna trails off incoherently, the doctor grasps her underlying mindset. He notes sympathetically that youth is given to illusions and that he sees sexual passion as Nature's "decoy" to secure mothers for the propagation of children. Dr. Mandelet adds that the passions given to us by Nature are on a level removed from moral considerations. Before parting, Doctor Mandelet tells Edna that she seems to be in trouble, and that if she would ever like to come to him for help, he would be a most understanding confidant. Edna responds that although she is sometimes upset, she does not like to speak of her despondency. She explains that she simply wants her own way, although she acknowledges the difficulty of this, especially when it means she must "trample upon the lives, the hearts, the prejudices of others." She asks the doctor not to blame her for anything, and he leaves, replying that he will blame her if she does not come to speak with him but that she should not blame herself, "whatever comes."

Edna sits on her porch, brooding over Adèle's final words, and vowing to think of her children the following day, after her rendezvous with Robert. To her dismay, Robert has left, and there is a note that reads, "I love you. Good-by—because I love you," in his place. Edna stretches out on the parlor sofa and lies awake all night.

SUMMARY: CHAPTER XXXIX

The next day, on Grand Isle, Victor and Mariequita flirt and discuss Edna's dinner party while Victor does construction work. Suddenly, they see Edna walking toward them. It is still long before the summer season, but Edna explains that she has come alone to the island in order to rest. She makes plans to have lunch with the pair and then walks down to the beach for a swim, ignoring Victor and Mariequita's claims that the water is much too cold. The night before, Edna had thought of her one desire, Robert, and how one day even he would disappear from her thoughts. She had thought of her indifference to Léonce. She had thought of her consideration for her children, whom she had begun to see were the only real shackle binding her soul to the slave-like existence she has led for so long.

As she walks along the beach, Edna's thoughts are completely different. She spies a bird with a broken wing flying erratically before crashing into the surf. She finds her old bathing suit, still hanging on its peg from the summer, and puts it on. Once she reaches the water, she removes the garment with no one in sight. For the first time in her life, Edna stands "naked in the open air, at the mercy of the sun, the breeze that beat upon her, and the waves that invited her." She feels like "some new-born creature, opening its eyes in a familiar world that it had never known." She swims out into the water without a glance backward, thinking of Léonce, of her children, of Robert, and of Mademoiselle Reisz's words: "The artist must possess the courageous soul that dares and defies." She thinks of Robert's note to her and muses that he had never understood her and never would—perhaps Doctor Mandelet would have, but now it is too late. Eventually exhaustion overtakes her, and memories of her childhood fill her thoughts as she surrenders to the expanse of the sea.

SUMMARY & ANALYSIS

Analysis: Chapters XXXVI–XXXIX

By the time Robert returns from Mexico, Edna has ceased to think of herself as a possession. Yet, Robert's abstention from Edna shows that he continues to understand male-female relations as those between a possessor and a possession. Robert's complaints of Edna's "cruelty" reveal that he doesn't see any way for the two of them to be together because he sees society as exerting an inescapable force. Robert does not perceive that Edna has not grasped this for herself and, thus, considers her continued pursuit of him to be intentionally malicious and vain.

Only when Edna and Robert finally speak honestly of their feelings for one another does Edna begin to undergo the tragic, final revelation of her awakening. Robert admits that he had fantasized about Edna becoming his wife, had harbored wild ideas of Léonce setting her free. He thus regards the central issue of his relationship with Edna to be the problem of ownership and the transfer of ownership—not the notion of love, or of simply being together. While Edna thought she could use her relationship with Robert to liberate herself from convention, and saw a life with him as one of the goals of her liberation, she now finds that to run to Robert is to run straight into the arms of the old male-female power dynamic.

Edna laughs at Robert's conventional views and scoffs at the idea of Robert claiming her as a possession. She tells him, "I am no longer one of Mr. Pontellier's possessions to dispose of or not . . . If he were to say, 'Here Robert, take her and be happy; she is yours,' I should laugh at both of you." Robert is shocked by the boldness of this statement, and perhaps also dismayed by the disregard it expresses for him and his own needs; Edna seems to mock Robert's profession of loyalty. Robert does not want a conventional affair, nor does he want to be just another step in a purely selfish quest for independence. Despite his love for Edna, he cannot respect her love for him if it can be realized only in adultery.

Yet Robert, too, feels passion. We read that Edna's "seductive voice, together with his great love for her, had enthralled his senses, had deprived him of every impulse but the longing to hold her and keep her." Thus, though he knows that the relationship cannot end as they wish, he begs her to stay. Robert's passion allows him some insight into Edna's own mindset but not enough: he feels torn between his love and his sense of moral rectitude, but his passion is not strong enough to make him decide in favor of his love. Edna does not fully realize this until she discovers Robert's note. When even Robert, whose love matches the sincerity and desperation of her own, refuses to trespass the boundaries of societal convention, Edna acknowledges the profundity of her solitude.

Edna realizes that she is still trapped, shackled to society and its expectations. What provides these shackles are not the men in her life but the boys. Her final despondency does not result from her fear that she will forever remain a dependent but from her thoughts of those who depend upon her. Thus, she says to herself, "To-day it is Arobin; to-morrow it will be some one else. It makes no difference to me, it doesn't matter about Léonce Pontellier—but Raoul and Etienne!" Edna has freed herself from Léonce, and she can avoid Robert if she thinks he would become similarly controlling. Her children, on the other hand, make her feel "overpowered." She imagines that by virtue of their very weakness, their vulnerability, their reliance upon her for their own reputation and social happiness, they seek "to drag her into the soul's slavery for the rest of her days." Edna's suicide affirms the claim she made to Adèle that for the sake of her children she would sacrifice her life but not herself. To return to her miserable marriage with Léonce for the sake of her children would be to betray the essence of her being. By killing herself, she avoids self-betrayal while still preserving her children's reputation. Indeed, Edna seems to have carefully arranged her suicide so as to make it appear an accident: by specifying to Victor that she will be lunching with him at the house, she ensures that he will believe she had intended to return from the water.

It is unclear whether Edna's suicide is meant to show her failure or her success. On the one hand, the suicide is an act of ultimate submission to the power of social mores. Instead of running away somewhere and living alone, perhaps supporting herself as an artist in the manner of Mademoiselle Reisz, Edna is able to think only of her sons' reputations and how they would be treated were she to leave. One could argue that such a surrender is generous—that Edna does not want to "trample on the little lives" of her sons and cause them pain. Equally convincing is the argument that the suicide is a cowardly rather than generous surrender, that an honest act of generosity on Edna's part would be to live on as an independent and strong woman, serving as an extraordinary example to her sons and thus helping them to undergo their own liberations.

The suicide can be also be seen as Edna's rebellious assertion of her own will: because Edna refuses to be tied down and to sacrifice "herself," she bravely sacrifices her life for the sake of maintaining her integrity and independence. By drowning herself, she ensures that her last act is a self-determined one.

The imagery in the novel's final passages underlines the ambiguity of its ending. We read that "a bird with a broken wing was beating the air above, reeling, fluttering, circling disabled down, down to the water." This description matches Mademoiselle Reisz's earlier warning, "The bird that would soar above the level plain of tradition and prejudice must have strong wings. It is a sad spectacle to see the weaklings bruised, exhausted, fluttering back to earth." If the bird Edna sees retains its earlier symbolism, then this vision is an indication of Edna's failure to transcend society and prejudice. If, the bird is a symbol of Victorian womanhood, then its fall represents the fall of convention achieved by Edna's suicide.

IMPORTANT QUOTATIONS EXPLAINED

QUOTATIONS

1. *In short, Mrs. Pontellier was beginning to realize her position in the universe as a human being, and to recognize her relations as an individual to the world within and about her. This may seem like a ponderous weight of wisdom to descend upon the soul of a young woman of twenty-eight—perhaps more wisdom than the Holy Ghost is usually pleased to vouchsafe to any woman.*

   But the beginning of things, of a world especially, is necessarily vague, tangled, chaotic, and exceedingly disturbing. How few of us ever emerge from such beginning! How many souls perish in its tumult!

   The voice of the sea is seductive; never ceasing, whispering, clamoring, murmuring, inviting the soul to wander for a spell in abysses of solitude; to lose itself in mazes of inward contemplation.

   The voice of the sea speaks to the soul. The touch of the sea is sensuous, enfolding the body in its soft, close embrace.

These lines from Chapter VI describe the beginning of Edna's process of awakening. Most of the concepts explored in the novel are mentioned in this passage: independence and solitude, self-discovery, intellectual maturation, and sexual desire and fulfillment. With the remark, "How few of us ever emerge from such beginning!" the narrator points out that Edna is unique in her willingness to embark upon her quest for autonomy, fulfillment, and self-discovery. Certainly, each new character that appears in the book only serves to highlight Edna's uniqueness. The narrator's subsequent remark, "How many souls perish in [the beginning's] tumult!" foreshadows the turmoil that will result from Edna's growing awareness. It seems to suggest that from the moment her awakening begins, Edna is marked for death. Additionally, the mention of the sea's sensual and inviting voice presages Edna's eventual suicide. The line that begins, "The voice of the sea . . ." is repeated almost verbatim just before Edna's death.

2. *She perceived that her will had blazed up, stubborn and
    resistant. She could not at that moment have done other
    than denied and resisted. She wondered if her husband had
    ever spoken to her like that before, and if she had submitted
    to his command. Of course she had; she remembered that
    she had. But she could not realize why or how she should
    have yielded, feeling as she then did.*

This passage is from Chapter XI of the novel. Edna has just returned
from her catalytic first swim and is lying in the porch hammock,
refusing her husband's entreaties to come inside to bed. For the first
time in her life, Edna does not, out of habit, yield to Léonce's com-
mand. Rather, she speaks against his control and does as she wishes.
The narrator highlights the fact that, as Edna's thoughts and emotions begin to change, she also becomes more self-aware and begins
to analyze her former behavior. Her distance from her former self is
emphasized by her inability to reconnect to her former mindset;
although Edna remembers having submitted to her husband's
authority in the past, she cannot re-create the logic that would have
led her to do such a thing, and her own past behavior seems alien
and incomprehensible.

QUOTATIONS

3. *"How many years have I slept?" she inquired. "The whole
    island seems changed. A new race of beings must have
    sprung up, leaving only you and me as past relics. How
    many ages ago did Madame Antoine and Tonie die? And
    when did our people from Grand Isle disappear from the
    earth?"*

These lines, which Edna speaks in Chapter XIII, reflect her desire to
be isolated with Robert and, thus, free from the restrictions of the
society that surrounds them. At the same time, her fantasy that she
and Robert have *already* been left alone as "past relics" evidences
the way that her new self-awareness has separated her—danger-
ously—from reality. Mentally, Edna is already living in her own isolated, island-like, mythical world. She has not yet fully
acknowledged her feelings for Robert, nor does she understand the
effect that her love for him will have on her life in the real world.
Indeed, the conditions that Edna describes in this daydream are the
only ones in which a relationship between Edna and Robert would
be possible. As long as they live within society, their love is unable to
overcome social convention and tradition.

4.	*The pigeon-house pleased her. It at once assumed the intimate character of a home, while she herself invested it with a charm which it reflected like a warm glow. There was with her a feeling of having descended in the social scale, with a corresponding sense of having risen in the spiritual. Every step which she took toward relieving herself from obligations added to her strength and expansion as an individual. She began to look with her own eyes; to see and to apprehend the deeper undercurrents of life. No longer was she content to "feed upon opinion" when her own soul had invited her.*

These lines, which are found in Chapter XXXII, chart Edna's growing independence. In part, Edna's strength comes from her rejection of her social role. Her new house is more modest, and its small size disallows the entertaining that was such a part of her former life. Consequently, Edna believes that independence and social rank form an inverse relationship; she has "descended in the social scale," but she has "risen in the spiritual." Ignoring the expectations of those around allows her to act in accordance to her own impulses and opinions.

Edna's association of strength and individual expansion with a total rupture from society seems somewhat erroneous. Ultimately, Edna defines herself according to her ability to disregard, rather than interact with, others. Her belief that independence and integration within society are diametrically opposed may underlie her tragic death at the end of the book because Edna leads herself to a profound solitude just at the moment when her sense of self is most acute. Perhaps, however, the society in which Edna lives does not allow her to integrate herself and remain independent. Because her society denies women the ability to think and act as individuals, a woman who asserts her own, differing set of hopes and dreams may end in an all-or-nothing bind.

QUOTATIONS

5. "*The years that are gone seem like dreams—if one might go on sleeping and dreaming—but to wake up and find—oh! well! Perhaps it is better to wake up after all, even to suffer, rather than to remain a dupe to illusions all one's life.*"

This quotation, drawn from a conversation Edna has with Doctor Mandelet in Chapter XXXVIII, may be considered the overarching message, or "moral," of *The Awakening*. Even though Edna's awakening leads her to suffer from the wisdom and self-awareness it affords her, the year of joy and understanding that accompanies this suffering is worth more to Edna than a lifetime of the semi-conscious submission that defined her former existence. According to Edna, to live with self-awareness, possessed and controlled only by one's own soul, offers an existence far richer than a life lived according to the restricting "illusions" that are imposed by the expectations of others.

KEY FACTS

FULL TITLE
The Awakening

AUTHOR
Kate Chopin

TYPE OF WORK
Novel

GENRE
Bildungsroman (novel of intellectual, spiritual or moral evolution); kunstlerroman (novel of artistic realization or development); shares elements of and is heavily influenced by the local color genre

LANGUAGE
English (frequently makes use of French language)

TIME AND PLACE WRITTEN
Written between 1897 and 1899 while Chopin was living in St. Louis

DATE OF FIRST PUBLICATION
1899

PUBLISHER
Herbert S. Stone and Co.

NARRATOR
Anonymous; seems to align with Chopin herself

POINT OF VIEW
The novel is narrated in the third person, but the narrator frequently makes clear her sympathy for and support of Edna.

TONE
For the most part, the tone is objective, although it occasionally reveals support for the female independence and sexual and emotional awareness symbolized in Edna's awakening.

TENSE
Immediate past

Setting (time)

The novel is set in 1899, at a time when the Industrial Revolution and the feminist movement were beginning to emerge yet were still overshadowed by the prevailing attitudes of the nineteenth century.

Setting (place)

The novel opens on Grand Isle, a popular summer vacation spot for wealthy Creoles from New Orleans. The second half of the novel is set in New Orleans, mainly in the Quartier Français, or French Quarter.

Protagonist

Edna Pontellier

Major Conflict

Once Edna embarks upon her quest for independence and self-fulfillment, she finds herself at odds with the expectations and conventions of society, which requires a married woman to subvert her own needs to those of her husband and children.

Rising Action

While Edna vacations at Grand Isle, several events initiate her awakening. Her candid conversations with Adèle remind her of her long-repressed passions; Robert Lebrun's flirtations with Edna cause her to desire more autonomy from her husband; and Mademoiselle Reisz's piano playing serves as artistic inspiration for Edna. At Grand Isle, Edna swims in the ocean for the first time, giving her the courage she needs to embark upon her journey of self-understanding and self-fulfillment.

Climax

The climax of *The Awakening* is difficult to ascertain, as Edna Pontellier's series of awakenings all possess a certain climactic quality. Most readers view Edna's suicide as the definitive climax of the novel. Other possibile climaxes include the first time Edna commits adultery by having sex with Alcée Arobin, and the moment when she declares her love aloud to Robert Lebrun and the two finally kiss.

Falling Action

The generally accepted climax of the novel is Edna's suicide at the end of the novel. In this case there would be no falling action. An alternative reading would suggest that the falling action is Edna's liberated and defiant behavior following her initial physical act of indiscretion—her affair with Arobin.

THEMES
Solitude as the consequence of independence; the implications of self-expression

MOTIFS
Music; children; houses

SYMBOLS
Birds; the sea

FORESHADOWING
The novel relies heavily on foreshadowing. Most examples pertain to Edna's rebellious and independent actions in the second half of the novel. In Chapter VIII, Adèle Ratignolle warns Robert that Edna, who is different from the other women on Grand Isle, may take his affections seriously. Adèle's concerns and Robert's impulsive reply that he indeed wishes Edna would take him seriously both presage the later romantic relations between the two. The lurking presence of the lady in black behind the young lovers suggests the tragic end that will come to the lovers' symbolic counterparts, Edna and Robert. Edna's suicide is foreshadowed countless times throughout the novel. The most obvious of these examples is Edna's rebellious swim in Chapter X. The surge of power and momentary vision of death Edna feels during this swim foreshadow her eventual suicide.

STUDY QUESTIONS & ESSAY TOPICS

STUDY QUESTIONS

1.   *What is the symbolic importance of the lady in black and of the two lovers? These characters often appear at the same points in the novel; what is the significance of this pairing?*

The lady in black represents the conventional Victorian ideal of the widowed woman. She does not embark on a life of independence after fulfilling her duties as a wife; instead, she devotes herself to the memory of her husband and, through religion, to his departed soul. If Léonce were to die, a widowed Edna would be expected to lead her life in such a socially acceptable manner. Edna longs for independence from her husband, but the lady in black embodies the only such independence that society accepts in women: the patient, resigned solitude of a widow. This solitude does not speak to any sort of strength of autonomy but rather to an ascetic, self-effacing withdrawal from life and passion. It is as though the widow's identity is entirely contingent upon her husband: the fact of his death means that she, too, must cease to experience the pleasures of life. Throughout the novel, this black-clad woman never speaks. Her lack of self-expression reinforces the lack of individuality underlying her self-governed but meaningless life.

The two young lovers are obvious mirrors of Robert and Edna, displaying the life they might have had together, had they met before Edna's marriage. At several points in the novel, the lady in black follows the young lovers. Her solitude and mourning symbolize the eventual failure of every union and, thus, the imminent failure of Robert and Edna's relationship.

QUESTIONS & ESSAYS

2.   *What is the symbolic meaning of Edna's first successful*
      attempt to swim?

Paradoxically, Edna's first swim symbolizes both rebirth and maturation. When she descends to the beach, she is described as a "little
tottering, stumbling, clutching child, who . . . walks for the first time
alone." Before her awakening, Edna is afraid of abandoning herself
to the sea's embrace, feeling an "ungovernable dread . . . when in the
water, unless there was a hand near by that might reach out and
reassure her." Early in *The Awakening,* the sea is described as
"seductive; never ceasing, whispering, clamoring, murmuring,
inviting the soul to wander for a spell in abysses of solitude; to lose
itself in mazes of inward contemplation." The sea represents truth
and loneliness, a vast expanse of solitude and vulnerability that
Edna has long been afraid to enter. Her relationship with Robert has
caused her to begin to develop and explore her own identity. As
Edna discovers for the first time her own power, she begins her rebellion. Her swim in the ocean shows that she is no longer dependent
on the help of others, as was expected of women, but instead finds
strength and support within herself.
    Before her rebirth, Edna was trapped in a perpetual childhood of
feminine dependency. When she realizes that she is, in fact, swimming, Edna shouts, "Think of the time I have lost splashing about
like a baby!" Edna's shout of triumph symbolizes her shedding of
the prolonged childhood forced on Victorian women. During the
first six years of her marriage, Edna had resisted Léonce's will only
in momentary spurts, always eventually conceding and conforming
to his authority. Now, however, she will no longer be ruled as a
child. Becoming reckless and over-confident, she wants to swim
"where no woman had swum before," and she reaches out "for the
unlimited in which to lose herself." She extends her arms and
explores the expanse of her new world.
    Edna's awakening is not complete with this swim though, for, look-
ing back, the distance to the shore seems to her "a barrier which her
unaided strength would never be able to overcome." Dread of death
seizes her and she realizes the flip side to independence: she can rely on
nothing but her own strength to get her back to safety. Her failed
attempt to swim far beyond the traditional waters of womanhood
implies that Edna does not have the staying power required to withstand the consequences of defying social conventions.

QUESTIONS & ESSAYS

One might read Edna's quick exhaustion in the water as a fore-shadowing of her death, which is brought about by a similar inability to fulfill her goal of transcending society. Or, her suicide may be read as her "completion" of her first swim. By the end of the novel, Edna comes to the realization that she has no place in the world around her, and her continued awakening and increasing acts of independence have given her the strength and courage she lacked during her first swim, the courage necessary to remove herself forever from the grasp of any other human being.

QUESTIONS & ESSAYS

3. *Early in* THE AWAKENING, *the narrator remarks that Léonce thinks of Edna as "the sole object of his existence." What evidence does the novel provide to support this declaration?*

While Léonce continually expresses devotion for his wife and concern for the well-being of his family, he seems to hold a double standard regarding his and Edna's respective roles in their marriage. Early in the novel, Léonce returns home late after a night at the club, but rather than allowing Edna to sleep, he insists on waking her to tell her about his evening. He expects her to perform the role of devoted audience, and yet earlier in the afternoon he had shown little interest in speaking with her, leaving to go to the club just after she had returned from her swim. It seems that Léonce invents a fictitious fever for one of their sons out of his annoyance with Edna's disinterest—Edna finds nothing wrong with Raoul when she checks on him. When Edna returns from her son's bedroom, Léonce proceeds to reproach her mothering skills. He upsets Edna and then falls asleep, leaving her to deal with her discontent on her own.

Though he means no harm in his treatment of Edna, Léonce is not entirely blameless. His sparse knowledge of his wife may be the result of his prioritization of work over family. During their summer vacation on Grand Isle, he spends the weekdays working in New Orleans, "eager to be gone" because he looks forward "to a lively week in Carondelet Street." Furthermore, he takes a long business trip when the family returns to New Orleans, despite having been concerned enough about Edna's behavior to warrant going to the doctor for advice. It is only in her husband's absence that Edna truly changes, discovering herself and the pleasures offered by others.

Because he sees Edna as a possession and not as an equal, Léonce never makes an effort to understand her feelings, nor does he seek out her opinion on any matters. Moreover, just as one might choose one's clothing or furnishings based on what they will "say" to others who see them, Léonce worries not about Edna herself, but about what others think of her and how this will reflect back on himself. He cares most about his social standing. For example, when Edna abandons her Tuesdays at home, Léonce warns her that she could jeopardize their place in high society instead of asking about the motivations behind Edna's actions. Similarly, when he learns that Edna plans to move out of the big house, he does not express concern for her decision to remove herself from the family home, a sym-

QUESTIONS & ESSAYS

bol of their marriage and relationship, but worries instead about what the move might suggest to others about his financial situation.

Thus while Léonce does dote upon his wife and works hard to bring money into the household, it is really only her material well-being and comfort that he makes the "sole object of his existence": he does not possess enough insight to worry about her emotional and psychological health. Indeed, insofar as Léonce regards Edna as a pretty pet and the finishing touch to the traditional household, one could read the above quote with a certain irony: for in Léonce's eyes, Edna is indeed an "object."

SUGGESTED ESSAY TOPICS

1. *How does the text use clothing and garments (or the lack thereof) to portray Edna's rebellion against Victorian norms?*

2. *Of the many awakenings Edna undergoes in the novel, which are most important to her progress? Which may be considered "rude" or unexpected awakenings?*

3. *Explore the full implications of the various images of birds in the novel. How do the different species of birds mentioned— parrots, mockingbirds, pigeons—symbolize different ideas?*

4. *Throughout the novel, Edna feels caught between the way others see her and the way she sees herself. Identify several moments in which this struggle is apparent. How does the text portray Edna's growing awareness of these contradicting views?*

5. *Some critics view Edna's suicide at the end of the novel as a failure to complete her escape from convention—an inability to defy society once stripped of the motivation of a man by her side. Others view her suicide as a final awakening, a decision to give herself to the sea in a show of strength and independence that defies social expectation. Which interpretation do you find more compelling, and why?*

REVIEW & RESOURCES

QUIZ

1. What is the name of the island on which the Pontelliers and
    other wealthy Creole families spend their summer vacation?

    A. Capri
    B. Grand Isle
    C. L'Isle de Paris
    D. Granada

2. What instrument does Mademoiselle Reisz play?

    A. The clarinet
    B. The flute
    C. The guitar
    D. The piano

3. What is the home Edna moves into in New Orleans called?

    A. The pigeon house
    B. The birdcage
    C. The House of Seven Gables
    D. La petite maison

4. Where does Edna go with Alcée Arobin and Mrs. Highcamp
    when Léonce is out of town on business?

    A. The opera
    B. Baton Rouge
    C. The racetrack
    D. Grand Isle

5. To what country does Robert Lebrun move?

    A. France
    B. Canada
    C. England
    D. Mexico

6. What does Victor Lebrun do to upset Edna at her dinner party?

    A. He chews with his mouth open
    B. He sings a song that reminds her of Robert
    C. He tries to seduce her
    D. He tells her that Robert is going away

7. What does Edna say she will not give up for her children?

    A. Her art
    B. Her life
    C. Her money
    D. Herself

8. How does Edna die?

    A. She allows herself to drown in the sea
    B. Léonce finds out about her infidelity and murders her
    C. She dies of old age
    D. She poisons herself at the Lebrun cottages

9. When Edna visits Adèle Ratignolle during her friend's difficult childbirth, what does Adèle tell her just before she leaves?

    A. To think of her husband
    B. To think of her children
    C. To think of the possibilities
    D. To think of Robert

10. Why did Edna's father and sister oppose her marriage to Léonce Pontellier?

    A. Because he was so much older than she
    B. Because he was a Creole
    C. Because he was a Catholic
    D. Because he was a not a Yankee

11. What is Edna expected to do every Tuesday afternoon at her home in New Orleans?

    A.   Speak with Mademoiselle Reisz
    B.   Have a painting lesson with Laidpore
    C.   Go to the Louisiana Women's Club meeting
    D.   Receive visitors

12. What is the phrase that Madame Lebrun's parrot repeats?

    A.   "Allez vous-en! Sapristi!"
    B.   "Venez ici, venez ici!"
    C.   "Voulez-vous coucher avec moi ce soir?"
    D.   "Ah! si tu savais!"

13. What do the Farival twins' parents intend them to do as adults?

    A.   Become lawyers
    B.   Marry rich husbands
    C.   Become famous pianists
    D.   Enter a convent

14. In what war did Edna's father, the Colonel, fight?

    A.   The Spanish-American War
    B.   World War I
    C.   The French and Indian War
    D.   The Civil War

15. What event does Edna refuse to attend, despite her father's pleadings?

    A.   Her mother's funeral
    B.   Her sister's wedding
    C.   Her child's piano recital
    D.   Her father's retirement ceremony

16. With whom does Edna converse on Grand Isle just before her death?

    A. Robert Lebrun
    B. Victor Lebrun
    C. Madame Lebrun
    D. The lady in black

17. Which of the following characters represents the Victorian ideal of the "mother-woman"?

    A. Mademoiselle Reisz
    B. Madame Lebrun
    C. Adèle Ratignolle
    D. The lady in black

18. With whom does Léonce Pontellier share his concerns about Edna's behavior?

    A. Doctor Mandelet
    B. Adèle Ratignolle
    C. God
    D. Mademoiselle Reisz

19. What object does Robert bring back from his trip that makes Edna jealous?

    A. A picture of his new wife
    B. A painting
    C. A parrot
    D. A tobacco pouch

20. What foreign language do the characters of the novel often interject into their dialogue?

    A. Spanish
    B. English
    C. French
    D. Latin

REVIEW & RESOURCES

21. What skill does Edna learn while vacationing at Grand Isle?

    A.   How to play the piano
    B.   How to swim
    C.   How to play tennis
    D.   How to paint

22. In what decade is the novel most likely set?

    A.   The 1790s
    B.   The 1920s
    C.   The 1890s
    D.   The 1850s

23. To whom does Robert write letters while he is away?

    A.   Mademoiselle Reisz
    B.   Adèle Ratignolle
    C.   Victor Lebrun
    D.   Edna

24. What does Léonce think when he notices Edna's rebellious behavior?

    A.   He decides she must be in love with another man
    B.   He suspects that she has been smoking opium
    C.   He wonders if she is going mad
    D.   He speculates that she is going through menopause

25. Where does Léonce often eat dinner?

    A.   At the home of Doctor Mandelet
    B.   At his men's social club
    C.   At a nearby Cajun restaurant
    D.   On the veranda

ANSWER KEY:

1: B; 2: D; 3: A; 4: C; 5: D; 6: B; 7: D; 8: A; 9: B; 10: C; 11:
D; 12: A; 13: D; 14: D; 15: B; 16: B; 17: C; 18: A; 19: D; 20:
C; 21: B; 22: C; 23: A; 24: C; 25: B

Suggestions for Further Reading

CULLEY, MARGO, ed. *The Awakening*. New York: W.W. Norton, 1994.

DYER, JOYCE. THE AWAKENING: *A Novel of Beginnings*. Twayne's Masterwork Studies 130. New York: Twayne, 1993.

HUF, LINDA. *A Portrait of the Artist as a Young Woman: The Writer as Heroine in American Literature*. New York: Frederick Ungar, 1983.

MARTIN, WENDY, ed. *New Essays on* THE AWAKENING. Cambridge: Cambridge University Press, 1988.

RANKIN, DANIEL. *Kate Chopin and her Creole Stories*. Philadelphia: University of Pennsylvania Press, 1932.

SEYERSTED, PER. *Kate Chopin: A Critical Biography*. Baton Rouge: Louisiana State University Press, 1969.

TOTH, EMILY. *Kate Chopin*. New York: Morrow, 1990.

SPARKNOTES
TEST PREPARATION
GUIDES

The SparkNotes team figured it was time to cut standardized tests
down to size. We've studied the tests for you, so that SparkNotes
test prep guides are:

Smarter:
Packed with critical-thinking skills and test-
taking strategies that will improve your score.

Better:
Fully up to date, covering all new features of the tests,
with study tips on every type of question.

Faster:
Our books cover exactly what you need to
know for the test. No more, no less.

SparkNotes Guide to the SAT & PSAT
SparkNotes Guide to the SAT & PSAT—Deluxe Internet Edition
SparkNotes Guide to the ACT
SparkNotes Guide to the ACT—Deluxe Internet Edition
SparkNotes Guide to the SAT II Writing
SparkNotes Guide to the SAT II U.S. History
SparkNotes Guide to the SAT II Math Ic
SparkNotes Guide to the SAT II Math IIc
SparkNotes Guide to the SAT II Biology
SparkNotes Guide to the SAT II Physics

SAT and PSAT are registered trademarks of the College Entrance Examination Board, which does not endorse these books.
ACT is a registered trademark of ACT, Inc. which neither sponsors nor endorses these books.

SparkNotes Literature Guides

1984
A Passage to India
The Adventures of
    Huckleberry Finn
The Aeneid
All Quiet on the
    Western Front
And Then There Were
    None
Angela's Ashes
Animal Farm
Anna Karenina
Anne of Green Gables
Anthem
Antony and Cleopatra
As I Lay Dying
As You Like It
The Awakening
The Bean Trees
The Bell Jar
Beloved
Beowulf
Billy Budd
Black Boy
Bless Me, Ultima
The Bluest Eye
Brave New World
The Brothers
    Karamazov
The Call of the Wild
Candide
The Canterbury Tales
Catch-22
The Catcher in the Rye
The Chocolate War
The Chosen
Cold Mountain
Cold Sassy Tree
The Color Purple
The Count of Monte
    Cristo
Crime and Punishment
The Crucible
Cry, the Beloved
    Country
Cyrano de Bergerac
Death of a Salesman
The Diary of a Young
    Girl

A Doll's House
Don Quixote
Dr. Faustus
Dr. Jekyll and Mr. Hyde
Dracula
Dune
Edith Hamilton's
    Mythology
Emma
Ethan Frome
Fahrenheit 451
Fallen Angels
A Farewell to Arms
Flowers for Algernon
The Fountainhead
Frankenstein
The Glass Menagerie
Gone With the Wind
The Good Earth
The Grapes of Wrath
Great Expectations
The Great Gatsby
Grendel
Gulliver's Travels
Hamlet
The Handmaid's Tale
Hard Times
Harry Potter and the
    Sorcerer's Stone
Heart of Darkness
Henry IV, Part I
Henry V
Hiroshima
The Hobbit
The House of Seven
    Gables
I Know Why the Caged
    Bird Sings
The Iliad
Inferno
Invisible Man
Jane Eyre
Johnny Tremain
The Joy Luck Club
Julius Caesar
The Jungle
The Killer Angels
King Lear

The Last of the
    Mohicans
Les Miserables
A Lesson Before Dying
The Little Prince
Little Women
Lord of the Flies
The Lord of the Rings
Macbeth
Madame Bovary
A Man for All Seasons
The Mayor of
    Casterbridge
The Merchant of Venice
A Midsummer Night's
    Dream
Moby Dick
Much Ado About
    Nothing
My Antonia
Narrative of the Life of
    Frederick Douglass
Native Son
The New Testament
Night
Notes from
    Underground
The Odyssey
Oedipus Trilogy
Of Mice and Men
The Old Man and the
    Sea
The Old Testament
Oliver Twist
The Once and Future
    King
One Flew Over the
    Cuckoo's Nest
One Hundred Years of
    Solitude
Othello
Our Town
The Outsiders
Paradise Lost
The Pearl
The Picture of Dorian
    Gray
Poe's Short Stories

A Portrait of the Artist
    as a Young Man
Pride and Prejudice
The Prince
A Raisin in the Sun
The Red Badge of
    Courage
The Republic
Richard III
Robinson Crusoe
Romeo and Juliet
Scarlet Letter
A Separate Peace
Silas Marner
Sir Gawain
Slaughterhouse-Five
Snow Falling on Cedars
Song of Solomon
The Sound and the Fury
Steppenwolf
The Stranger
Streetcar Named
    Desire
The Sun Also Rises
A Tale of Two Cities
The Taming of the
    Shrew
The Tempest
Tess of the d'Ubervilles
The Things They
    Carried
Their Eyes Were
    Watching God
Things Fall Apart
To Kill a Mockingbird
To the Lighthouse
Tom Sawyer
Treasure Island
Twelfth Night
Ulysses
Uncle Tom's Cabin
Walden
War and Peace
Wuthering Heights
A Yellow Raft in Blue
    Water